Hoax

Also by Nicholas von Hoffman

Mississippi Notebook, 1964

The Multiversity, 1966

We Are the People Our Parents Warned Us Against, 1968

Two, Three, Many More, 1969

Left at the Post, 1970

Fireside Watergate
(with Garry Trudeau), 1973,

Tales from the Margaret Mead Taproom
(with Garry Trudeau), 1976

Make Believe Presidents, 1978

Organized Crimes, 1984

Citizen Cohn, 1988

Capitalist Fools, 1992

HOAX

WHY AMERICANS ARE SUCKERED BY WHITE HOUSE LIES

Nicholas von Hoffman

NATION BOOKS
NEW YORK

HOAX: *Why Americans Are Suckered by White House Lies*

Copyright © 2004 by Nicholas von Hoffman

Published by
Nation Books
An Imprint of Avalon Publishing Group
245 West 17th St., 11th Floor
New York, NY 10011

Nation Books is a co-publishing venture of the Nation Institute and
Avalon Publishing Group Incorporated.

Library of Congress Cataloging-in-Publication Data is available.

ISBN 1-56025-582-X

9 8 7 6 5 4 3 2 1

Book design by Simon M. Sullivan
Printed in the United States of America
Distributed by Publishers Group West

To my son
Sgt. Aristodemos von Hoffman, United States Army,
presently on active duty in Iraq

"The genius of you Americans is that you never make clear-cut stupid moves, only complicated stupid moves."

—GAMAL ABDEL NASSER, 1918–1970,
President of Egypt and the
(defunct) United Arab Republic.

Contents

Hoax

1.
The Big Lie

THE FRIGHTENING SHARK SWIMMING with toothy grin in a giant aquarium does not see the human faces looking in from the other side of the glass. The shark is in a world of its own, with its own reality. Like the shark, Americans don't see the people outside the glass. It is as though America is in a 3,000 mile wide terrarium, an immense biosphere which has cut it off from the rest of the world and left it to pick its own way down the path of history. By the time the American army stepped into Iraq, the difference in world view between the United States and everybody else had grown to the size of the hole in the atmosphere over the South Pole.

A fanciful explanation for the two realities is that the United States is the continent-wide set for a large scale re-enactment of the movie *The Truman Show*. The plot of that movie has the well-intentioned but naive hero go about his daily life without any suspicion that he is, in fact, in a gigantic soap opera. His hometown is actually the set for the TV show and from earliest childhood he has been manipulated and controlled by the producer and the director. The enthusiastic acceptance by the American multitudes of the Iraqi stuff-and-nonsense coming out of the White House would be understandable if we all are living on a stage set in a village called Freedom Island threatened by a town called Evil Axis.

Americans believed, as they usually do when their government and their television tell them something, but the rest of the world laughed every time George Bush or Colin Powell or Dick Cheney or Donald Rumsfeld thought up yet one more scary reason to invade Iraq. The ill-constructed, clumsy untruths were surprisingly crude for people who have had years to practice the craft of mass deception, and they had only to speak their latest falsehood to be cheered by their countrymen and disbelieved by non-Americans everywhere.

It's not easy to pull off the Big Lie and George Bush failed; though, in mitigation, pulling off a bait-and-switch war demands skillful finagling and this one was complicated. There was the bait (terrorism), then the switch (weapons of mass destruction), then a switch again (kill the dictator), and yet again (regime change). A politician has to be an accomplished teller of tall tales and absurd fibulations to bring off such a demarché. Even the masters of mass prevarication occasionally fail.

In September 1939, Adolf Hitler made the mistake of

dressing up some nondescript clowns in Polish uniforms and having them "attack" the territory of the Third Reich. This was done to show an incredulous world that his invasion of Poland, which quickly followed his costume party on the border, was a justified counter thrust to unprovoked aggression. The world didn't believe him, but Hitler didn't care. At Obersalzberg, just before initiating the hell which was World War II, he had announced that, "The . . . destruction of Poland begins Saturday early. I shall let a few companies in Polish uniform attack in Upper Silesia. . . . Whether the world believes it is quite indifferent. The world believes only in success." Hitler, the Biggest of Big Liars, had the brass and the disdain which George Bush, under his Texas cowpuncher veneer, does not have. This may be to his credit, but without them Iraq was guaranteed to be a bloody mess. If you are going to tell a Big Lie badly, you have to pull off the crime, you have to make it a success. George Bush didn't.

The Big Lie must be simple and it must be repeated until it reverberates like a jack hammer digging up the street in front of where you live: inescapable sound. George Bush, either out of a fumbling honesty, inexperience, or incompetence, did not lie well. His labored and embarrassing build-up to the Iraqi invasion broke every rule for effective deception.

Unlike a chef d'état who has the technique down pat, Bush made the amateur's mistake. He, his spokesmen and women, his spinners and weavers of untruth, his propagandists, all fell into the trap of answering back, elaborating, retracting, and adding on. Instead of the Big Lie, simple and pure, the official U. S. government story grew more ornate and complicated as the date Bush had set for the invasion came closer. Instead of one good reason to go to war, swarms of bad reasons were proffered, which gave skeptics in other countries material to pick his little white fables apart.

A corollary to keeping things simple is to refrain from offering evidence. Where there is no evidence there can be no refutation. Bush, however, trumpeted that he had warehouses full of evidence—which, as it happened, consisted of tons of used paper towels and soiled Kleenex. Once exposed to air and light, the truckloads of proof positive turned into proof negative; the often-cited smoking gun was revealed to be a dribbling water pistol.

The more evidence the world's last remaining superpower brought forth, the goofier or more dangerous Mr. Bush appeared to foreigners, who saw him as either a gibbering bobble-head doll or an international menace. In one of the UN's more memorable afternoons, the world heard American Secretary of State Colin Powell, who a year earlier had said that Saddam was toothless and "has not developed any significant capability with respect to weapons of mass destruction," explain to the Security Council that a photograph of what looked like a couple of rusty, abandoned Good Humor ice cream trucks actually showed traveling war germ factories. The ice cream trucks, he told his global audience, many of whom must have been rolling on the floor laughing, were making biological weapons of mass destruction.

Heaping Pelion on Ossa, the secretary of state pulled another photograph out of his attache case. This one, he said, was of an Iraqi pilotless airplane bearing Saddam Hussein's weapons of deadly germs and lethal chemicals, ready for takeoff. To the non-American part of his audience the object looked like the balsa wood airplanes boys glue together and fly in the park. After the model airplanes and the ice cream trucks came the aluminum tubes for the non-existent atom bomb factories, forged documents out of Africa, tales of spies and agents meeting in Viennese cafes, far-fetched dribs and super-secret drabs of what was hopefully called intelligence. The more of it Powell and Bush gave the world, the less the world believed.

Mexican President Vincente Fox and Canadian Prime Minister Jean Chretien were having none of George Bush's mega-fibs. The United Kingdom, the other partner in the Coalition of the Willing—a phrase the White House tunesmiths must wish they could take back—was dragged into the Iraqi adventure over the protests of millions of its indignant subjects by a prime minister whose consecration to the Anglo-American "special relationship" almost destroyed his career. When it came to foreign politicians rallying to the American cause, there were few Bush could count on, though he had the support of Ariel Sharon, a man who has never seen an Arab he didn't want to throttle, and Silvio Berlusconi, the Italian premier/businessman shunned as a crook and white collar criminal by all of Europe.

Nevertheless, the voluble Silvio had a way of expressing

the less-than-articulate George Bush's thoughts: "We must be aware of the superiority of our civilization, a system that has guaranteed well-being, respect for human rights—and in contrast with Islamic countries—respect for religious and political rights, a system that has as its values understandings of diversity and tolerance," said the enthusiastic premier, who on another occasion explained the difference between Saddam Hussein and one of Premier Berlusconi's predecessors in the office by remarking that, "Mussolini never killed anyone . . . Mussolini sent people on holiday to confine them [banishment to small islands such as Ponza and Maddalena which are now plush resorts]." Not that the ordinary Italians were rushing to the colors. The idea that Saddam Hussein was an immediate threat to anybody but his own people was disbelieved there and everywhere except in the United States.

There is something distant and abstract about a term like "weapons of mass destruction." You can see how the fear that they might exist could make a lot of people give George Bush and his fellow doomsayers the benefit of the doubt. After all, who's to say that Saddam, being the homicidal swine he is, might not have had a few poison-gas rockets capable of killing people in Israel or even farther afield?

But for most of the world such ruminations and nugatory suspicions did not add up to a case for invasion. Why then did Americans go for it, embracing the preposterous assertion that Saddam Hussein, however malevolent his intentions may have been and however nauseating his past acts, was a fearsomely powerful chieftain able to strike a meaningful blow against the United States?

You didn't have to be a retired general to know it couldn't be. Twelve years before, the American armed forces had demolished the Iraqi military. They had done it in 100 hours of shelling, bombing, and shooting at Saddam's army—which did fight back. Before the 100-hour massacre, American air power had spent days destroying the Iraqi electric power, public utilities, and transportation facilities. After the 100-hour war, if you want to dignify the 1991 skirmish with that name, a United Nations commission had destroyed Saddam's poison gas, his biologicals, his rickety, inaccurate rockets, and the poor beginnings of a nuclear weapons program. Since then the Americans and the British had—sometimes periodically and sometimes incessantly—bombed whatever Saddam had left in the way of fighting forces.

The defeated—though always devious—dictator had no means of rebuilding the inferior force which had been destroyed in 1991 when he was driven out of Kuwait. After Gulf War I, the United States, through the UN, controlled the sale of Iraqi oil which, other than rugs, was that country's only significant source of income. The United States, again through the UN, decided what and how much Iraq could buy with the little moneys allotted to it. It was scarcely permitted food and medicine. As for guns, perish the thought. Embargoes and sanctions aside, the money wasn't there to pay for the war machine the United States insisted Saddam had but was hiding among the camels. The

Iraqi nation was prostrate, as innumerable visitors, returning home after seeing Baghdad's hungry children, reported. It was ludicrous to suppose that the dictator and his two sadistic sons posed a threat to anyone other than those unlucky enough to be Iraqi citizens.

What was obvious to others wasn't to Americans. They nursed the thought that people in the rest of the world might not have taken Saddam Hussein to be the toothless tyrant he was if 9/11 had happened to them. If the French and the Germans had seen three thousand of their people murdered in one blow, if they had had a personal experience with terror it might have made them less lenient with a man like the Bastard of Baghdad. A man who, whatever the evidence or the lack thereof, had something to do with the destruction of the World Trade Center; who, you may be sure, was in cahoots with al Qaeda; who, have no doubt about it, was slipping money to fanatic Muslim militants; who could let go forty-five minutes after the command of an immediate missile attack against the United States in the spring of 2003. What was received as subjective theorizing in Europe was flat-out fact in the United States. America and the rest of world were veering away from each other.

The horror of 9/11 had been met with enormous sympathy abroad, but it did not cause people elsewhere to take leave of their senses. None had lost 3,000 people in one blow to terrorist attacks, but the American sense of the uniqueness of what their country had suffered was not taken by others to be a license to go berserk and act like a bull wildly kicking its hind legs and expelling rockets from its nostrils in every direction across the globe. Not even non-Muslim India, which has over the years endured assassinations and terror attacks rivaling or surpassing America's suffering, approved. The Russians, committed to a struggle in which their horrors are answered with a terrorism as appalling as any, could not bring themselves to go along with the invasion of Iraq. Why couldn't America see it? And why is this question so seldom asked?

2.
Desert Mirage

OW COULD THE PENTAGON AND THE White House believe that if they invaded Iraq they would be met with armed resistance? Did they really think the Iraqis were able or willing to fight a war? "War" is being used here in the ordinary definition of two armies, guerilla or regular, no matter how disproportionate in size and strength, who at least pretend to fight for a day or two before the stronger wins. For example, the periodic conflicts over the last half-century between the Israelis and the Arabs can be called wars, even though they always end quickly with the Arabs getting their butts kicked. One-sided though they may be, for a brief period of time you may justifiably say that two military organizations met in combat. That's a war.

The government fostered the illusion, after the American army's tourist excursion to Baghdad, that there had been a war, replete with heroes, gritty bravery and derring-do. But in reality the American passage of arms in Iraq was no more than a drive-by shooting, the kind that is supposed to transpire every night in Los Angeles. There was no war. There was an occupation akin to the American occupations of Grenada under President Reagan or Panama under the first President Bush, or Adolf Hitler's waltz into the Rhineland in 1936. The invasion of Afghanistan, however sad its eventual consequences have turned out to be, can be classified as a war. The Afghans shot back in something approaching an organized fashion. They weren't good at it and in no time at all the business began to look like a pheasant shoot or a fox hunt, but it was a war. There was an enemy, they had guns, they could use them, and they did—as compared with Iraq which, despite the hoo-hah over weapons of mass destruction, had the fire power of the Indianapolis, Indiana, Police Department.

Did Powell, Rumsfeld, the New European, Wolfowitz, Bush, Rove and the other members of the Patriotic Circle believe that there was an Iraqi army? Or did they know better but, since there could be no selling an invasion or war on an obviously impotent Iraq, did they conjure up an Iraqi war machine out of the undulating hot air currents of the desert? Was there a little mirage-making going on? Did they repeat their "weapons of mass destruction" demarche with a similar exaggeration of Iraq's ordinary military capabilities? Did they know that there would be no Third Gulf War because the putative foe did not have the wherewithal for battle and had not even prepared to fight? Did they know that Iraq lay naked in front of the American army, which could drive in and take it at will?

The scariest answer to these questions is no, they didn't know. It is possible that these men, with the world's most gigantic and elaborate military and intelligence apparatus at their disposal, got it wrong. It is possible that they are fools, that first they terrified themselves with bogeymen and then terrified their people. We can hope that Bush et al did lie, manipulate, and deceive. Rather a clever knave than an honest fool. If they didn't lie, if the people who hate George Bush because they believe that he is evil, selfish, and mean are mistaken and he turns out to be one of history's disastrous idiots, there is no predicting the outcome to the long tragedy which is the Middle East.

With its satellites and the rest of what is called "technical means," which, one has to suppose, means a network of spies and espionage agents, the United States had to know that, despite Saddam's strutting, Iraq's military organization was incapable of resisting anything more formidable than a small group of men mounted on camels armed with spears and scimitars. Assuming that, on account of some extraordinary lapse, the never-fallible intelligence agencies did not realize that there was no enemy army to make war on, the figures in command might have learned the true state of affairs had they stepped outside the Pentagon and the White House and bought a newspaper. They could have read in the *Washington Post* the following pre-invasion dispatch from Baghdad:

> Baath Party members, some middle aged with paunches stretching their green uniforms, manned sandbagged positions built over the past two weeks and patrolled

streets throughout the city. Most were armed with AK-47 assault rifles . . . Blue-uniformed police at intersections wore helmets and took up assault rifles, and small knots of soldiers were spotted wandering around the city . . . But tanks, artillery and even troop movements were nowhere to be seen.

As the American army pursued its joyride toward Baghdad, incidents of violence were surprisingly rare. As more American service personnel met their deaths from accidentally being run over by Coca-Cola delivery trucks than from hostile fire, it ought to have become apparent to officialdom and even the public at large that things were not quite as advertised. It did not. With each day of the invasion the absence of fighting did not become either a publicly commented-on puzzle or the source of political embarrassment. The invasion was a war wearing the Emperor's New Clothes.

Washington had an explanation for the first phase of the war that wasn't: Saddam was planning a horrific, Muslim Gotterdammerung in the fabled capital city of the Fertile Crescent. The dictator had drawn his forces back to Baghdad in preparation for turning the city into a desert Stalingrad, where ugly street battles and house-to-house fighting would cost the lives of many soldiers and civilians.

It was all stuff and nonsense. Readers of the *Washington Post* knew such a thing was not in the cards. Evidently they knew before the Pentagon that Baghdad would fall without a shot to the first Humvee with enough gasoline to drive into the center city. As the Americans bounced along from the south and the west toward Baghdad, the *Post* gave this description of the preparations for the city's defense: "The four- and six-lane highways that radiate to the south and west are more burdened with pickups carrying onions and garlic than transports ferrying troops to the front. A scattering of checkpoints, pillboxes and sandbags mark the city's entrances—a barren landscape interspersed with factories and groves of date palms and apricots. The sentries go largely unnoticed by children playing soccer in dirt fields and women in black chadors selling tomatoes and eggplant on straw mats along the street.

"On the strategic road from Karbala, a concrete arch bears the inscription, 'Baghdad welcomes you.' "

In the air war, the Americans briefed the world's press on how they had gained mastery of the skies thanks to their incomparable superiority, which is certainly true enough, but it is also true that power was not tested. In reality, the United States didn't win the air war over Iraq. There was no air war over Iraq. For the first and perhaps the only time in the history of aerial warfare an air force met its adversary by going to ground, as this from the *Los Angeles Times* explains: " 'The only order I got was to dismantle my airplanes—the most idiotic order I ever received,' said Brig. Gen. Baha Ali Nasr, 42, an air force commander who said Iraq's entire fleet of MIG-23s, MIG-25s and Mirage fighters was ordered taken apart and buried. Dirt and grime in the pits and berms where the planes were buried ensured that they would never be airworthy again, he said." Did those U.S. satellites which

were able to inventory the popsicles in Saddam's Good
Humor trucks fail to see the holes being dug to bury what
was once the French- and Soviet-supplied Iraqi air force? Is
that believable? When the losses were totaled up, the numbers revealed that the United States lost more troops at the
hands of Sitting Bull at the Battle of Little Big Horn than it
did at the hands of Saddam Hussein in Gulf War III.

The victory won, President Bush celebrated this passage
of arms by famously descending onto the deck of one of his
aircraft carriers where he walked about in brave array. Never
was he more the Commander in Chief than in his aviator
suit, bowlegged from his oversized cod piece, proclaiming
the end of a war which was never fought to seize a cache of
weapons of mass destruction which didn't exist. From
Maine to California, from Alaska to Florida, millions
cheered and nary a tree or a porch post escaped its red,
white, and blue ribbon.

3.

The American Biosphere

THE SEPARATION BETWEEN THE American view and the world view over the recourse to violence has been apparent for years and long antedates the division over attacking Iraq. As nation after nation—Arab, among some other nations, excepted—has given up the death penalty, America, though it once toyed with the idea of abolishing it, has taken it up again with a zeal not seen since the early part of the 20th century. Then-Governor Bill Clinton broke off campaigning in New England in 1992 to fly home to Arkansas to preside over the execution of a half-wit to propitiate popular opinion. If not with relish, then with general approbation, Governor George Bush saw hundreds of his own people into the Texas death-operating room where the condemned are killed with chemicals but not in the wholesale manner of Saddam Hussein. Elsewhere a close career connection with the taking of life would exclude a politician from attaining the highest offices; in the United States it is a recommendation. While in other places the death penalty is reserved for the rarest and most heinous crimes, the American Congress attaches it to ever more transgressions.

The cult of the gun, incomprehensible to people from other lands, flourishes in America. Man and boy, pistol and phallus, the modern American is ready to ride wild stallions in the contest against universal evil. The gun-slinging avatar astonishes visitors, but no more so than the one or even two hundred million firearms which are said to be floating around the United States, or the more than two million people in jails and penitentiaries—which to foreign eyes have the look of an American-style luxury Gulag. However great the admiration for American accomplishments—and both the accomplishments and the foreign admiration thereof are enormous—the United States has become a strange land where the traditional values and beliefs once shared with the western world have undergone a subtle shift.

Every national state of any size has its own unique culture formed by myths, history, needs, and beliefs. Norwegians and Greeks do not see the world in the same terms, but the consequences of those disparities are probably not even important to Norwegians and Greeks. They are not walled off from each other by unbridgeable dissimilarities. Indians and Pakistanis don't appear to exist in different realities, either. Not that it does them much good, but they can understand each other and communicate. They simply disagree—to the point of violence and past it—because they both want the same piece of Kashmiri real estate and are willing to kill for it.

The person who hails from a national biosphere containing its own reality is convinced that the person from outside the biosphere is wrong about everything. Wrong values, wrong perspective, wrong morals, wrong beliefs, wrong across the board. That is how the Communists saw the world before they lost faith in their system. It was a characteristic of the Germans seventy years ago. Having a different reality is not the same as having a disagreement with an *auslander*.

Nineteen-thirties Germany was under its own glass dome. Outside the Teutonic biosphere Adolf Hitler was a small, silly man with a brush moustache in a trench coat, jumping up and down and screaming at the top of his voice, making an utter ass of himself; a comic character in deportment though not in content. To the Germans of that era there was nothing ridiculous about him. Inside the German biosphere he came across as a strong man talking common sense truth. He was the leader—Der Fuhrer—and it was very unfunny. A different reality.

For many a German, Nazism was not dictatorial. It was the very spirit of liberation. It was freedom. It was jobs. And talk about endowing people with a sense of empowerment! Political enslavement comes in the native clothes of one's own biosphere. It is disguised. If the Judeo-Christian fascism creeping about the edges of the American englobement were to take power it would not be wearing jackboots. You will see none of the gorgeous uniforms they put on the Nazis in the movies intended to show how bad they were but ending up displaying how good they looked. No heel clicking. No Nazi salutes. American fascism, if it were to take over, would be decked out in familiar, Southwestern shit-kicker cowboy boots. Our Gestapo would wear blue jeans and shop at Sam's Club. If it were to come, it would be good old boy fascism, informal and friendly, with the perpetual, goofy smile Americans decorate their faces with. People would not know it had happened. Americans would still think that they were living in a democracy. Only the other people, the ones outside the glass, would see what had gone on. Were they to tell their American friends, the American friends would not believe them.

America in the 2000s has nothing in common with the Nazi Germany of seventy years ago except that it, too, is under a transparent globe. The faunae in the American biosphere have no resemblance to the venomous wildlife of early 20th-century fascism, but the terrarium explains the development of a peculiar American view of reality which estranges, frightens and puzzles old friends and close allies. When America insists its citizens must be exempted from the jurisdiction of the International Criminal Court, an institution dedicated to the enforcement of basic human rights laws, the United States is making a statement about itself. Its stance betokens a conviction that Americans are so special they should not be judged as others are, and that is the work product of a different reality.

The others outside the biosphere see and take note. They form opinions. In a survey taken after the Anglo-Saxon invasion of Iraq, thirty percent of Germans under the age of 30 believe it is possible that the United States government itself ordered up the 9/11 attack. What else must they think of a government which they believe might have been capable of killing 3,000 of its own people in order to set up a persuasive reason for going to war? The unique claims America makes for itself are heard, and they widen the divide between America and those who ought to be friends and collaborators.

Nations are often imbued with the belief that they are special, but the American credo holds that the U.S. is special-*special*. Belief in a unique national story and narrative generally comes out of a woolly myth from the distant past, such as the twin brothers who were mothered by a wolf and ended up founding Rome, or the Jewish god who gave his people the land of Israel. But unlike nations that base their identity on ancient writings like the Norse sagas, America's belief in the nation's special destiny arises from what people have done in relatively recent history. The American legacy does not depend on believing improbable-sounding stuff which may or may not have happened thousands of years ago. America's faith in its being different, special, one-of-a-kind, and chosen by God comes from real men and women whose portraits hang on the walls of the nation's patriotic shrines. The foundations of the American socio-political biosphere date from them.

4.
That City on That Hill

THE ROOTS OF AMERICAN particularism, the conviction of a nation set apart, goes back three hundred years. It begins even before the Puritans docked. In 1630, John Cotton told the Mayflower pilgrims before they boarded their little ship that they were God touched. "I will appoint a place for my people Israel, and I will plant them, that they may dwell in a place of their own, and move no more . . ." [II Samuel 7:10] was his text, but the reverend embroidered on his theme in a way which was to echo through the centuries down to our own time.

"Wherein doth this work of God stand in appointing a place for a people?" he asked the congregation which was about to sail off to the wilds of North America. Answering his own question he said, ". . . when God espies a land for a people . . . that is when, He gives them to discover it themselves, or hears of it discovered by others . . . After He hath

espied it . . . He carrieth them along to it, so that they plainly
see that a providence of God leading them . . . So that
though they met many difficulties, yet He carried them high
above them all, like an eagle, flying over seas and rocks. . . ."

What if somebody else is living on the God-appointed
camping grounds? John Cotton had an answer to that question. "God makes room . . ." the minister explained, ". . . He
casts out the enemies of a people by lawful war with the
inhabitants . . . "

But this course of warring against others and driving
them out without provocation depends upon special commission from God. . . . War without provocation or preemptive warfare is moral war if God approves and, since God
carried the European Englishmen to the New World, by that
act He gave His sign of His approval and, evidently, has
never withdrawn it.

The only other nuclear power claiming a special license
from the divinity is Israel. The Israeli divine patent goes back
five thousand years, which makes the American claim seem
almost trivial. But it is no less ardently held, as is reflected in
every other sound bite by every other politician standing in
front of the Capitol looking into the TV cameras.

American particularity was not an eccentricity on John
Cotton's part. That sense of being an elect was expressed at
the same time, 1630, by John Winthrop, who arrived in the
Massachusetts Bay Colony immediately after the
Mayflower. "We shall find that the God of Israel is among
us," he wrote, "and ten of us shall be able to resist a thousand of our enemies. The Lord will make our name a praise

and glory, so men shall say of succeeding plantations, 'The Lord make it like that of New England.' For we must consider that we shall be like a City upon a Hill; the eyes of all people are upon us."

The city on a hill is a place established by God. The conviction that the United States is God-based, faith-based, and chosen of heaven persists undiminished. It gives Americans that special *oomph* they have whenever they tell anyone and everyone "We are right and you are wrong." It cannot be otherwise, for Providence has chosen America to work through human history. The municipality on the hill is the social culmination of God's plan.

The belief that America was to be the cynosure of the world begins almost two centuries before the government of the United States was established. It burrowed into the culture and consciousness of these ex-Europeans from the start of their North American adventure. Twenty years later, in 1651, the hill metaphor was being used by the Reverend Peter Bulkley in a sermon in which he explains to his flock that, "And for ourselves here, the people of New England, we should in a special manner labor to shine forth in holiness above other people ... We are as a city set upon a hill, in the open view of all the earth, the eyes of the world are upon us, because we profess ourselves to be a people in covenant with God ..."

These Puritan divines hit the mark. What would become the United States did become the admiration of the world, though less for its religiosity than for its high standard of living and even, from time to time, for the freedom of its people. Four hundred years later presidents were still up on the hill. Ronald Reagan, in his 1981 inaugural address, used the phrase, saying that "every dawn" would "be a great new beginning for America," and that "every evening" would bring us "closer to that shining city upon a hill."

The city was more than a tourist attraction to the countless speakers who have used the metaphor. For many of them it meant that America should be a model and an example, but others bend the meaning. "We should in a special manner labor to shine forth in holiness above other people," the preacher said. In the passage of time the sentence was seemingly altered to read, "We should in a special manner labor to shine forth above other people." The holiness was still implicitly there, running in the background, supplying rationalizations for all manner of public acts which reeked of everything but the odor of sanctity.

A people who had been specially recognized by Him, Who liveth and reigneth forever, soon came to believe that they had also been given heavenly letters of marque, sanctioning their theft of other people's real estate. The proof that the Lord had blessed them with permission to occupy the universe was famously enunciated by a John O'Sullivan. In 1845, he coined an expression Americans would use for decades afterwards, as if it were a divine outward sign that they had permission to steal land which did not belong to them. Urging the impending filching of Texas from Mexico, O'Sullivan explained that it was no more than living up to "our manifest destiny to overspread the continent allotted by Providence for the free development of yearly multiplying millions." A manifest destiny of a people or a nation must, obviously, only come from on high. The phrase was so self-validating. Anyone with eyes to read a map could see that the fledgling United States was manifestly destined to occupy the continent. It was still the city set on the hill, but it was a big hill and an expanding city.

In addition to enabling Americans to give themselves permission to go about taking what belonged to others, the phrase "manifest destiny" reaffirmed the nation's specialness. It had the tenor of religiosity which backs up American claims and ambitions to this day. Fifty years after O'Sullivan, that self-same presumption of God-givenness shows up in an 1895 article by Senator Henry Cabot Lodge, a major political figure at the turn of the 20th century. Cock-a-doodle-doing over the nation's growth, he turns George Washington, of all people, into an Old Testament figure— and perfumes his text with familiar religious animadversions—when he writes that Washington, ". . . saw, with prophetic vision, . . . the true course of the American people. He could not himself enter into the promised land, but he showed it to his people, stretching from the Blue Ridge to the Pacific Ocean. We have followed the teachings of Washington. We have taken the great valley of the Mississippi and pressed on beyond the Sierras. We have a record of conquest, colonization and territorial expansion unequaled by any people in the 19th century." Spoken in pride, not shame.

"The record of conquest," etc., was achieved without serious European interference thanks to a mother country whose fleet, as powerful then in relation to the rest of the

world as the American fleet is now, shooed everybody else
away from American shores. The special Anglo-Saxon relationship did not spring up at once after the War of 1812.
There were ups and downs and little spats between Great
Britain and her wayward child throughout the 19th century,
but the affinities between the two English-speaking powers
drew them closer with each passing year. Using the American house of Morgan as a conduit, English investors put up
much of the money to build the American railroad system.
British interest in American prosperity assured the young
republic a free field to gain its destiny while the rest of
Europe could either lump it or invest too, which is what the
Germans did.

Lodge's kind of talk, delivered by the most prestigious figures, was dinned into the population for decade after decade.
You hear it long enough, you begin to believe it. "Fellow
Americans, we are God's chosen people," Senator Albert J.
Beveridge of Indiana, a famous orator in his day, proclaimed
in an 1898 campaign speech. "It is a mighty people that He
has planted on this soil," he went on. "A people imperial by
virtue of their power, by right of their institutions, by authority
of their Heaven-directed purposes..." If you make allowances
for Beveridge having been more literate and more energetic
than George W. Bush and/or his speech writers, the same
sentiments and the same grasp of reality are in the words of
both men.

In time the idea of America as the instrument of Providence elaborated itself. The United States was not merely
one nation, more or less like other nations, which God for

His reasons had chosen to work through, but His instrument, as in the New Testament text where Jesus says, "You are Peter and on this rock, I found my church." The political institutions were infused with religious meaning. There built up over time a fantasy of America as a religious edifice. For the millions, high- and low-income, this set of ideas has become more than a metaphor. It's as real as church on Sunday.

Early American history—the most important figures of the Federalist period and its principle documents—were incorporated into a sacramental system. Symbolically and emotionally those crackly 18th-century parchments, the Declaration of Independence and the Constitution, have been turned into Holy Writ. The texts of the documents are treated as sacred writings, the material on which shoals of Talmudist professors and lawyers feed and use to instruct the multitudes about the immutable religious truths of a political system which must be ever revered and never changed, not by one Biblical jot nor proverbial tittle. As monks once disputed in monasteries, constitutional theologians now argue over the Signers' and the Framers' real meanings, when those ancient worthies, guided by the all-wise spirit, put goose quill to sheepskin more than two centuries ago. Not only did they bring forth a government, but also a secular religion.

It was a long time, however, before everybody sat in the pews of this church. African-Americans lined up to join but were not admitted, while millions of Roman Catholic immigrants from a dozen or more nations were reluctant to join.

Catholicism is an elected monarchy which has a deep antipathy to democracy, let alone a form of Calvinist Protestantism disguised as a secular government. The American Catholic church split over accommodating itself to the secular religion. In 1899 Pope Leo XIII published an apostolic letter, *Testem Benevolentiae,* condemning "Americanism," meaning getting too close to the insidious secular religion begun by Washington, Jefferson, and the other members of the American Protestant Enlightenment. In due course Catholics, with their parochial schools, learned that they could hold on to their faith and turn the political weapons of the Protestant master class against their inventors. Catholicism slipped into the pews and prospered. The American Left—socialists, communists, anarchists and trade unionists— did not join the church. Its members prospered but its organizations and political parties vanished into a forgotten past and into a present confined to the classrooms of a few cranky, impassioned political science professors.

The Signers and the Framers have been assigned positions in the political-cultural life of the country like those of the Prophets and the Apostles. Their lives, their letters, and their published writings are scrutinized and re-scrutinized. Their personal property, their autographs, every artifact connected with them is treated less like an item of historical record and more like saints' relics. George Washington has, over the course of time, been upped from Father of His Country to God the Father. The Jesus figure is Abraham Lincoln, who died for America's sins, and the Paraclete seems to be a revolving office alternately held by the Adams family and Thomas Jefferson—although since Jefferson has been accused (or exposed or revealed or suspected or say-what-you-will) of having an illicit sexual relationship with a slave woman he has faded somewhat into the background of the American pantheon.

The American religion or the religion of Americanism (the un-Catholic kind) is not the same as the ordinary god-is-on-our-side-ism which seizes all tribes, clans, peoples and nations when they go to war. The religion of America operates in peace just as well as it operates in war because it's not a simple jumping up and down, jingoistic war cry. It's a reigning faith and, though it derives from a Christian paradigm, it has proven to be syncretic enough to get Hindus, Jews, Muslims and Sikhs, and people of any other religious tradition to buy into it.

As faiths go, this is not an arduous one. Heaven on earth is promised to the devotees in the form of the American Dream, and little is asked of the faithful save that they emit patriotic yelps and yells when bidden. Although much is said about sacrifice for your country, few in the pews are forced to do much of it (if you don't count the income tax as a sacrifice). There having been no military conscription for almost two generations, only those well into middle age remember being threatened by the possibility of some serious, mandatory sacrificing. In a prosperous and happy land where want is unknown and the word has no real meaning, the practitioners of the American religion have little asked of them as they wax fat and occasionally complain about the price of gasoline. And wax fat is *le mot just* in a country where obesity and *avoir du pois*—and the gaining and losing thereof, with their ramifications for health, future income, life expectancy and satisfactory sexual congress—take up more television time and magazine pages than Iraq. The motto of the American religion might as well be "little is demanded and less is expected." Yet for all the cushiness of the American credo, it is the foundation for and major contributing factor to the psychotic break that has resulted in the nation's diminished capacity to share the same reality with the other inhabitants of the globe.

5.
Flag Waving

FLAGOLATRY, OR THE EXCESSIVE or demented reverence for the national symbol, has its innocent roots in the first lines of the National Anthem. Then things began to get out of hand. Respect for the flag commenced to become flagolatry, part of the degraded and antic patriotism which distorts what, in saner hands, are decent and praiseworthy feelings for one's country. That country was hardly born before people started running Old Glory up the flag pole with a vengeance. The tendency to overdo turns up in Joseph Rodman Drake (1795–1820), who gave his compatriots "The American Flag":

> Flag of the seas! On ocean wave
> Thy stars shall glitter o'er the brave;
> When death, careering on the gale,
> Sweeps darkly round the bellied sail,

And frightened waves rush wildly back
Before the broadsides reeling rack,
Each dying wanderer of the sea
Shall look at once to heaven and thee,
And Smile to see thy splendors fly
In triumph o'er his closing eye.

Such thoughts, standing alone and taken one at a time, are not necessarily to be criticized. After all, the Roman poet, Horace, said much the same thing a couple thousand years ago when he wrote, "Dolce et decorum est pro patria mori," or "it's sweet and right to give your life for your country." Some flag waving is good, a lot of flag waving is tolerable, incessant flag waving is crazy and dangerous and easily manipulated by the war party to get people bubbling at the mouth in fear and rage.

By the time of the Spanish-American War, a conflict which has been described as "squalid," flagolatry had become a national mental disorder. That little war inspired Henry Holcomb Bennett to write "The Flag Goes By," the refrain of which is:

Hats off!
Along the street there comes
A blare of bugles, a ruffle of drums:
And loyal hearts are beating high:
Hats off!
The flag is passing by!

Mr. Bennett's patriotic poesy is mouldering with many another offering of the same stamp, but some have passed the test of time. In 1906 George M. Cohan brought forth "You're a Grand Old Flag," a toe-tapping ditty which even sullen American anti-bellicists cannot completely resist. Cohan, who did for belly-up-to-the-bar, six-pack patriotism what the self-starter did for the automobile, cannot fairly be blamed for the intolerant, flag-waving jingoism which grows like ragweed in the American terrarium, but he did supply pathological patriotism with a hymnal full of danceable, singable songs.

Military patriotism in other countries has its repertory of rousers which have the same unfortunately intoxicating effect on those who sing them. Very little critical thinking is going on when a person, in the company of ten thousand other vocalizing fools, is singing his head off as he marches forward toward some thrilling abstraction. Unless one knows the words and their import, it is hard even today to be unmoved by the "Horst Wessel Lied," the Nazi anthem:

Flag high, ranks closed,
The S.A. marches with silent solid steps.
. . . .
Millions, full of hope, look up at the swastika;
The day breaks for freedom and for bread.

Note the use of the word "freedom," George Bush's favorite noun. Everything depends on the context, of course, so when we see pictures of Bush backgrounded by rows and rows of American flags, the type of photo op that Adolf Hitler also favored, a second look helps before judgment is formed. Nevertheless, when you see the President make an appearance before a flag-draped mise-en-scene which might have been prepared by Leni Riefenstahl, the theatrical genius who made Hitler's rallies so hypnotically compelling, all the bunting does not make for a smarter, wiser or more generous-minded leader. Rhetoricians have a term of art for this kind of manipulating of emotion and mind. It's called *ad captandum vulgus*, which loosely translates into "bamboozling the moron masses with showy irrationalities." Politicians like Bush who do it have an ingrained contempt for the people they lead, so asking them to take a higher road is a waste of time. It is up to the masses of moron manipulatees to de-moronize themselves by using their noodles.

In America, flag-fetishism goes back at least a hundred and twenty years. There are photographs of the 1896 presidential campaign showing thousands of people marching up Fifth Avenue in New York, each holding his own red, white, and blue. Nevertheless, when flagalotry takes over the landscape, as it has in the last generation, it says something about people who dwell in that country. Not only does every unpaid-for, overly-mortgaged house in the United States boast its own copy of Old Glory, but so does every SUV, every truck, every truck stop, the side of every barn. The men wear flags in their lapels and, given the propensity of contemporary youth to insert their jewelry into their flesh,

God alone knows where they are flying their flags. China and the nations which have supplanted the domestic textile industry may be confused by the demand but must be delighted by the raging need in the United States for more, ever more *drapeaux*.

As if the flag needed a boost, it got one anyway in 1892 when the Pledge of Allegiance first saw the light of day. It was intended for public school children but now everyone must recite it at every conceivable function. Failure to utter the words can result in falling under suspicion. Suspicion of what? Well may you ask, but you'll not get an answer.

Although the man who wrote the Pledge, Francis Bellamy, was some kind of utopian socialist and a Baptist minister to boot, he didn't seem to have thought of the Pledge as a patriotic blackjack to whack the small minority of the unenthused and unconvinced into appearing to support stringent methods and strident patriotism. This corporal's guard of nay-sayers—or at least nay-thinkers—understands that standing at attention and unthinkingly reciting words whenever one is told to do so is either ridiculous or imbecilic or an obedience drill for a people already susceptible to group think.

Flagism is accompanied by anthemism. You're lucky if you can get through a day in the United States without having to come to attention, place hand on heart and listen to its anthem once or twice. There is no place, no time and no occasion when it is deemed unseemly to full throttle into "Oh, say can you see . . ." At some baseball games it is sung twice, although why it should be sung at all at such an event is inexplicable. For those of us not trained in grand opera, the song is next to unsingable unless the singer is drunk, a condition which enables the possessors of ordinary voices to believe that they have negotiated the tune—and avoid thinking of the politics behind it. At some baseball games they hit you with the National Anthem at the start and then you get the more singable "God Bless America" in the seventh inning. "This Land Is Your Land" is played less often. Is it because its lyrics have an irenic quality to them or because the song was written by a Communist or because it has a loosey-goosey, we-can-all-join-in melody which is counter to the spirit of tight-assed discipline? Patriotism wants a tromp-tromp-tromp, not an amble-amble-mee-amble.

I suppose that the purpose of flag display is inspirational, but taken together with allegiance-pledging and such, its effect is stifling, confining, and intimidating. It was used for the same purpose in the months leading up to America's entry into World War I. An electric sign was strung across New York City's 5th Avenue in 1916 flashing the orders for "Absolute and Unqualified Loyalty to Our Country." In a society of lapel pin flags and standing to attention and red, white, and bluing, the uninterruptedly repeated message is don't talk, listen up, and get ready to rumble. The overall effect is not yet that of the totalitarian state, but to visitors from abroad, what's going on here has a different and worrisome cast from what they do back home in Sweden or Holland or Portugal. Everywhere in the United States are the signs and symbols of military nationalism.

Loud, pot-banging nationalism has long been an American

trait. Whether it is more raucous than it was a hundred years ago would be impossible to say, inasmuch as displays of nationalism then were as ear splitting to sensitive spirits as they are now, but in 1903 it was a characteristic shared by the people of all the major military powers of the world. Everybody was singing their version of the 1878 British music hall song from which the word jingoism derives:

> "We don't want to fight: but if we do, by Jingo,
> "We've got the ships, we've got the men, and got the money, too!"

In the Western world at least, nationalism, particularly the armed, bullying kind, swept up every country with pretensions to being the proprietor of a military force. The end of Emil Zola's novel *Nana* gives us a taste of the masses coursing through the streets of 1870 Europe ecstatic and crazy mad for the witless war which would soon consume them. The photographs of the generals and admirals of the period illustrate the bristling chauvinism intoxicating everyone. There they are, the commanders, literally with feathers and plumes in their hats, the medals on their chests effulgent, boots and sabers gleaming, doing their nationalistic turkey struts. Nationalism, aka patriotism, led the way toward the unmitigated catastrophe which was World War I.

After which came World War II, an even more unmitigated catastrophe in which fifty million or more died, a hecatomb to racism, fascism, communism, the love of country, and faith in the resort to weapons of mass destruction. But nationalism was on the wane. A comparison of World I and World War II posters, cartoons, and music reveals how nationalism, with its romantic heroism, had been drained out of the second global conflict. World War II posters have none of the mystical, superhuman warrior figures of World War I. The people in the World War II iconography are down to earth types trying to get a hateful job done. The archetypal American soldiers are Willie and Joe, two grungy cartoon infantry men who hate the war and their commanding officers. The Tyrtaean tunes redolent with martial glory of the first war have given way to ballads of longing and loneliness. If World War I's "Over There" made the blood surge, World War II's "Lilli Marlene" made the heart break. A German song, which the Nazis tried to suppress in favor of marching music, "Lilli Marlene" is said to have been translated and sung by soldiers in no less than forty-eight languages:

Underneath the lantern,
By the barrack gate
Darling I remember
The way you used to wait
T'was there that you whispered tenderly,
That you loved me,
You'd always be,
My Lilli of the Lamplight,
My own Lilli Marlene.

Until the late 1970s nationalist fervor declined in America as well as Europe. This was the time of the Cold War, which was conducted primarily on ideological, not nationalistic, lines. For the free countries, the hallmark of their foreign policies, the United States included, was the sublimation of nationalistic urges into cooperation. The United States was the *primus inter pares*, the first among somewhat equal nations, which freely gave admiring deference to the great republic in a network of voluntary international alliances and working agreements. In some places, however, after the dissolution of Communism the old nationalistic and communitarian passions flared hot again. Half the Balkans was destroyed in a recrudescence of nationalistic xenophobia, but the rest of Europe was untouched. The ancient nationalist furies in the largest countries of Europe continued to recede. As they did, Europe moved in one direction, the United States in another.

In France, Germany, Spain, Italy, and Scandinavia, nationalism was on the wane and was being replaced by political and economic forms of cooperation on such a large scale and in such detailed articulation that the grandparents of living Europeans would have said such things were utopian impossibilities. The nations of Western Europe had begun a process of union, not as a result of a conquest by a Charlemagne or a Napoleon, and not in reaction to the threat of an outside enemy, be it the Turks at the gates of Vienna or the Reds in Berlin. Immemorially old qualities of national personality, national character, or national interest which described the Dutchman, the Swede, the Spaniard, the German, Frenchman, Italian, etc., began to soften at least to the extent that these people found more and more things to share and do in common. Europe was no longer merely a word designating an area on the map; now it referred to a political and economic unity. If Euroman had not yet come out to stand on the stage of history, the nations in the Union were exchanging sovereignty for membership in a supranational federation. At the same time in America disgust, anger, contempt, and ignorance of and resistance against any organization asking nations to pool their sovereignty for any kind of common good grew.

Patriotism was getting dialed up. Politicians and their pilot fish swimming in the think-tanks denounced the "Vietnam syndrome," by which they meant the wrongness of looking before leaping or shooting second and asking questions first. Then in 1979, during the Jimmy Carter administration, a wild crowd of Iranian students and religious hop heads took American embassy personnel hostage and refused to let them go. The drama in Teheran, which dominated life in the White House and television for more than a year, set off surges of nationalism which have not yet stopped breaking across America. In the United States every tree, every vertical post was decorated with a ribbon making one kind of patriotic statement or another. The nation was sheathed and swathed in flags. When a stupidly conceived and poorly planned attempt to rescue the hostages crapped out in the middle of the desert, the jingoes took over the stage in American public life and have not relinquished it.

The world's reality and the ongoing reality under the terrarium's glass roof were at right angle disagreement. While hundreds of millions continued to admire America for its wealth, the opportunities it affords its people, and its individual liberties, usually in that order, the discerning visitor from abroad looked around and could see that the country was living in a permanent political fugue state.

6.
Democracies Are Always in the Right

I N THE BIOSPHERE THE belief is that any government certified as democratic is OK. Say no more, case closed because democracy confers a moral infallibility on the societies which have it. There is another apothegm, attributed to everybody from Winston Churchill to George Santayana, to the effect that democracy is a terrible form of government, yet it is just better than any other form yet devised. In that vein we are occasionally reminded that Adolf Hitler did not come to power via a beer hall putsch but through a valid constitutional process in what was, before he put an end to it, a free and democratic Germany.

Democracies are always in the right, the United States is a democracy, therefore the United States is always right. Added to the syllogism is the belief that, since America is the best democracy, it is righter than other democracies.

With this conviction as a first premise, further thought on a wide variety of topics is unnecessary. No need to collect information, sift it and think about it. Under this dispensation it is not even a question of my country, right or wrong, but my country, always right and never wrong.

Definitions of right and wrong are subject to change according to political need or the shifting standards of one generation or another. These days it goes without saying that democracies or republics protect the weak, oppose bullies, and are nice guys internationally speaking. The finance ministers of more than a few lesser developed or undeveloped countries, both democratic and tyrannical, might have a different take on the world's leading democracies' banking and trade practices. Leaving that nettlesome set of controversies aside, history is replete with stories of some rather unpleasant or pushy or greedy democracies.

The Republic of Venice, which at one point had quite a decent little empire of its own, spent centuries warring with its competitors for turf and trading privileges. It took its part in the wars and conspiracies waged among the republican city-states of the Italian Renaissance. So much for the maxim that democracies do not fight each other. Like our own republic, the Venetian Republic was immersed for centuries in an off-again-on-again relationship with the Muslim world during which deals were made, deals were broken, crusades and jihads were proclaimed and forgotten, wars were fought, and wars were ended as it suited the various parties. Present-day American maneuvering over Middle

Eastern oil follows patterns similar to the amoral, pragmatic tacking and weaving which comprised the Roman Catholic Venetians' relations with the unbelieving Ottoman Turks. That particular Muslim-Christian contest climaxed with Venice's epochal navy victory over the infidels at the battle of Lepanto in 1571.

By way of contrast, the current struggle against the Muslim menace is what the Pentagon calls "asymmetrical," meaning that the buggers in Iraq are hiding behind the sand dunes, practicing a form of guerilla warfare which makes a repetition of Lepanto impossible. You see, the Arab doesn't fight fair; that is, he will not stand up straight and honest so that superior American fire power can have its way. In as much as the Americans in their revolution subjected the British to pretty much the same treatment, their indignation over such terrorist tactics may be a trifle misplaced.

In the 17th century the doughty Protestant burghers of the Netherlands rose up and fought their way to freedom from Spanish Catholic suzerainty. The muscular Dutch Republic, among other acts of brigandage, seized for itself a gigantic colonial empire comprising all of the present day Indonesian archipelago, now a nation of some 200 million people. By the standards of the 1600s such acts did not make the Dutch Republic especially wicked or wicked at all. The English monarchy was doing the same or more. Likewise the French. Democratic or republican forms of government in and of themselves do not impel behavior which rises above the contemporary levels of virtue. In the 17th century invading somebody else's country, kicking out the native rulers, and more or less enslaving the population while pillaging the people was quite *comme il faut*. Subsequently, such carryings-on by democracies or anybody else fell into disfavor, but now the neoconservative faction in Washington is trying to make empire-building respectable again, as long as those doing it have good motives and a sincere desire to help the subject people.

7.
America Will Never Be the First to Use the Bomb

AMERICANS, AMERICANS BELIEVE, HAVE a unique reverence for human life and fair play. Others, of course, care for life and treating people with tender kindness—but not like we do. It's one more element which makes life inside the terrarium different from what goes on out there, where people like Saddam do terrible things to their own people and other people; where the French and Germans see, shrug, and turn away.

If a public opinion survey were to ask a question like "Would America ever drop the bomb first?", count on it, a healthy fraction of the respondents would say, "Never did, never will." Regardless of whether the United States should or should not have dropped the atomic bomb on two Japanese cities, there is a part of the population who do not know it happened, and if told about it, will soon not know it happened again. Dropping atomic bombs has no place in the American gestalt. Every time the event is written on the national conscience the palimpsest of memory wipes it out and writes some good deed of the heart in its place. From the outside looking in, you might say it was a case of disassociative political morality.

The national gestalt has it that America is the land of the warm and fuzzy. America is the birthplace of Donald Duck, Miss Piggy, Barney, and Mickey Mouse, endearing creatures without reproductive organs or sweat glands. Americans believe they are the most ardent dog and cat owners in the world. Americans also believe they love their children the most, referring to them as "kids," a word used to denote a special love foreigners do not have for their offspring. Mothers are called "moms," another gooey word suggesting unique American love, care and protection. Spanking or physical punishment is not permitted in schools. There are special, almost *sharia*-like, laws against touching other persons in those bodily places or any places. Doctors are required to report suspicious-looking bruises on a child. A crime committed against a child's person, especially if a child's person is a white person—blond is even better—will set off an indignant, horrified, national hullabaloo which may go on for days or weeks. Wife-beating, once a more or less tolerated Saturday night leisure time activity, is now suppressed and punished. In America, as nowhere else in the world, networks of institutions exist to enforce warm, fuzzy and safe. Whether daily life in this sense is better under the great American Astrodome than in Belgium or Japan or any other nation with a comparable per capita income is a subject for cultural psychiatry.

The word "abuse" has been elevated from being just an ordinary word sitting in the dictionary with its fellow words to being a kingpin word, applied to the widest range of behaviors. Recognized and punishable forms of abuse include parent-child, boss-worker, worker-worker, young-old, teacher-student, child-child, priest-acolyte, and clerk-customer relationships. How do I abuse thee? Let me count the ways. You cannot, for there are too many in a country which goes wild at the utterance of the word.

In the terrarium strictures against abuse take in speech as well. Slurs, hate speech, insults, jokes tasty and tasteless, snide remarks, and passing sarcasms directed against any congeries of people having some kind of recognition as an official or quasi-official group is subject to punishment. In the terrarium the body is protected from insult and so is the spirit, which befits a society which invented touchy-feely, for this is the land of fun and feel good. America is a nation of psychiatrists, therapists, psychologists, counselors and happy pills.

Against all of this goodness running in the background are tales past and present of social crimes of violence and community cruelty. Those with the ears to listen can hear stories of events like the Trail of Tears, that uprooting of Native American families, communities, and nations and their transplantation a thousand miles to the west, as if they were nothing more than a bunch of Arabs. The not-so-warm and fuzzy President Andrew Jackson may occasionally be quoted on the subject: "What good man would prefer a country covered with forests and ranged by a few thousand savages to our extensive republic, studded with cities, towns and prosperous farms . . . and filled with all the blessings of liberty, civilization and religion? . . . May we not hope, therefore, that all good citizens, and none more zealously than those who think the Indians oppressed . . . will unite in attempting to open the eyes of those children of the forest to their true condition, and by a speedy removal relieve them from all . . . evils . . ."

From time to time the morality of having dropped the atom bomb becomes a topic of discussion across the mass media and, after the arguments which have been used often before are used again to no effect, attention moves on to another debate topic. But the doubt remains, the question stays unsettled, the conscience is troubled, and every year on August 6th when the quiet bell is carefully struck at Hiroshima, a few stand and ponder. Somewhere in excess of 135,000 people perished at Hiroshima and Nagasaki. They are remembered in some fashion, but a half a million Iraqi children, dead by the American embargo on food and medicine, are seldom remembered inside the American biosphere. They are gone.

If the findings of the World Health Organization, the Food and Agriculture Organization and the United Nations International Children's Emergency Fund are accepted, the figure for the number of Iraqi children killed by the Anglo-American blockade may rise to 675,000. Although these numbers are not disputed, assume they are exaggerated by as much as fifty percent. That would mean "only" 250,000 or 300,000 or so children met their deaths by the starvation forced upon them by the Anglo-Saxon powers, so called because this thing was the work of the United States and Britain in the name of the United Nations, whose other members could not stop it. There were hundreds of thousands of adult deaths as well, but the fate of the children is already more than America has been able to face up to.

Far from owning up to what was done, the deluded inhabitants of the terrarium believe they have invented a novel, humane form of warfare, if that is not a contradiction in terms. In an article in *Foreign Affairs* called "The New American Way of War," Max Boot, one of the loudest of the pot-walloping Neocons, writes that, "Spurred by dramatic advances in information technology, the U.S. military has adopted a new style of warfare that eschews the bloody slogging matches of old. It seeks a quick victory with minimal casualties on both sides." Mickey Mouse and Barney go to war, nobody smells, nobody poops, and nobody dies.

An indignant Nancy E. Soderberg, a member of Bill Clinton's National Security Council, huffed at a *New York Times* writer that, "I could not give a speech anywhere in the U.S. without someone getting up and accusing me of being responsible for the deaths of 500,000 Iraqi children." If not she, who? She was way up there in the foreign affairs/national security apparatus of the Clinton administration.

The annoyances Ms. Soderberg was forced to endure are rare. Today's government officials, guarded by flak jacketed bodyguards, more often than not appear before audiences pureed and sieved for docility and assent. They are protected from close-up contact with the faces of dissent spitting insults at them. Broad, loud, and public dissent is rare. Americans, as do the cannon fodder elsewhere, trot meekly into the abattoir of war. It was not until the Vietnam conflict had been going on as long as the Siege of Troy that the college boy would-be conscripts broke into open rebellion at the prospect of being dropped into the Southeast Asian flesh-shredding machine. The only large scale, anti-war dissent in the 20th century occurred in opposition to World War I, but it was crushed soon enough.

Ms. Soderberg has escaped responsibility as has her boss, President Clinton, who signed the Iraqi Liberation Act. Although he probably will get the blame some day, they ought not to hang the fate of the formerly alive kids on Bush, who has enough of his own to answer for. But in reality, Ms. Soderberg can go unharassed. The dead children are not in the national memory, which accounts for the American astonishment that the Iraqi welcome to the invaders from across the seas was somewhat ambivalent.

Under the dome there are support groups for the parents of murdered children and special provisions for them to testify at the trials of their murderers. Iraqi parents must bear their grief in unassisted despair without professionally trained and licensed grief counselors. They must go it alone with none of the wide spectrum of mood altering drugs available to American parents stricken at the deaths of their small ones. But such are the advantages of living in a level-playing-field democracy.

James Rubin, Madeleine Albright's flak, when queried about all those dead little bodies, answered a question with a question, "What should we have done, just lift sanctions and hope for the best? I believed then and believe now that that was just too risky, given Saddam Hussein's past, his repeated attempts to invade his neighbors, his treatment of his own people and the weapons we knew he was developing." A bit of prevarication here. During the years of the children's death agony, there were no weapons of mass destruction and Saddam's "repeated" attempts to invade his neighbors are two in number, the first being his U.S.–backed invasion of Iran and the second being his theft of Kuwait, which he did on his own. Not that it excuses Saddam, but in the opinion of more than one historian, the reason he invaded Kuwait was the debts to Kuwait which he piled up in his war against Iran. His treatment of his own people deserves to put him in the dock at a war crimes trial, but he did not kill a half a million of them—though he killed more than a half a million Iranians, which does not seem to count when the Rubin types make their speeches.

"What should we have done, just lift sanctions and hope for the best?" Rubin asks. The answer, of course, must be yes, if not lifting the sanctions is tantamount to murdering half a million children. Right off the bat, most of us would be hard pressed to come up with any reason for killing a child, and as for half a million of them, that's for Mr. Rubin to mull over. The children died of starvation and diseases like dysentery for which there are treatments if the medicine is available, but the medicine was embargoed. Some day, perhaps even in a court of law, Clinton himself, and associates like Rubin and Soderberg, should be asked why and how keeping medicine from children would slow down Saddam's development of the non-existent weapons of mass destruction.

Most secretaries of state complete their time in office without forming a single, memorable syllable, but one remark by Madeleine Albright will not soon be forgotten. After being asked by a television reporter, "More than five hundred thousand Iraqi children are already dead as a direct result of the U.N. sanctions . . . Do you think the price is worth paying?" Albright answered that, "It is a difficult question, but, yes, we think the price is worth it."

When it dawned on her some years later that her price-is-worth-it remark might remind some people of Ilse Koch, the Bitch of Buchenwald, Albright told the *New York Times,* "It was a genuinely stupid thing to say . . . I wish people understood that these are not black and white choices; the choices are really hard." She regretted the remark but not the deed. What's vivid to the woman is her pain, for she goes on to say, "What was so terrible for me was that I did see the faces of the people who were suffering—even if I thought then and think now that the sufferings of the Iraqi people were Saddam's doing, not ours . . . No one had thought they would be in place for so long, but then, no one had really thought Saddam Hussein would still be there either. The intelligence was that he'd be gone fairly soon."

They were in place for so long. With each week bringing 6,000 or more children's deaths, still, it was not too long for Madame Albright. As per usual the intelligence agencies' projections of the future were goofy, stupid, and inaccurate so the blame lay elsewhere. Anyway, it was Saddam's fault. That's one of the old saws officialdom relies on. He brought it on himself. Blame him. But that Saddam or Castro was the reason or the cause of sanctions is not the same as Saddam doing the sanctions. It was the Americans' doing. It was their decision to drop the starvation bomb and the epidemic bomb, weapons which only cause collateral damage. Only the innocent, only the small fry, only the children, only the aged suffer and die.

Did Clinton and Albright think they were depriving Saddam of food? One look at his belly in his own propaganda pictures makes it clear that he was getting his three squares. Did they think if he got sick, his tame slaves would not rustle up medicine for him? She says that she saw "the faces of the people who were suffering." Did she believe that Saddam would see "the faces of the people who were suffering," and it would melt his heart, this appalling human being who was as bad as his enemies painted him? She says it was terrible for her. Do you believe that? Can you believe that it was terrible for her, yet she stayed the course, knowing the children were dying and knowing it had no effect on Saddam? The people who did see the children's faces resigned in protest. People like Dennis Halliday, head of the UN Office of Humanitarian Coordination in Iraq.

Albright saw the suffering faces. Bill Clinton felt your pain, felt their pain, felt everybody's pain, felt the throbbing pain of the universe, yet ultimately, in the last analysis, at the place where the buck stops, what happened to the children is what President Clinton willed would happen to them. In

September of 2003 he appeared at a burial site near Sre-
brenica where 7,000 Muslim men were murdered at the
same time the children were perishing in Iraq. The massacre, he said, oblivious to the irony of his words, ". . . laid
bare for all the world to see the vulnerability of ordinary
people to the dark claims of religion and ethnic superiority.
Bad people who lusted for power killed these good people
simply because of who they were." As for the children, it is
as though they were never born. Clinton is enthusiastically
received wherever he goes for he is this handsome, white
haired man of gentle manner, Bible in hand, speaking con-
soling words, confirming that America will never drop the
bomb first. He has made himself into the grotesque simu-
lacrum of a warm and fuzzy stuffed animal.

What would Albright have said if she had been told by
the Pentagon that they could drop a bomb on Iraq which
would absolutely kill Saddam but also half a million children? She would have to say the price was worth it,
wouldn't she? The truth is that if the collateral damage,
killing the children, is done out of sight of the TV cameras,
the price is worth it. But if the collateral damage is a photo-
genic, bombed-out building with dead people inside and
hysterical survivors outside, then the price is not worth it.

In the cockeyed reality which Americans daily breathe,
you can murder, if that's not too strong a word, the children
and simultaneously give elaborate demonstrations of smart
bombs which are so accurate that they almost never cause a
civilian death. As befits a nation hipped on teddy bears and
other soft, cuddly things, those miraculous bombs, and the

scrupulous care with which they are aimed, have convinced everyone under the crystal dome that America fights with a humane, "surgical" precision. One of the descriptions of how these children died would convince even a Madeleine Albright that a fast death from a dumb bomb is better than the slow death the children died. The Americans do their pinpoint bombing on camera and they do their starvation bombing off camera. Is this hypocrisy or schizophrenia?

8.
A Pax Americana on Us All

MERICAN TALKING HEADS ARE big on ancient Rome. In the sealed crystal palace of the unreal where they live, Rome is both an example of what can happen to a republic that gets off the straight and narrow, and a source of ideas to be copied. The Roman Republic, burdened not with a bicameral but a tricameral legislature and not one but two presidents who served alternate months, operated under a political system even more unresponsively rigid than the one in Washington, D.C., which may be why politicians and right-wing wonks are attracted to it. This ancient democratically based republic had little compunction about waging war on other republics or/and monarchies, tyrannies or any other form of government which got in its way. If there were a Jurassic Park wherein dwell extinct societies, a chance encounter by present day Americans with a cohort or two of Roman citizen soldiers would scare the hell out of us moderns. We are talking human T-rexes here.

These were tough hombres, tough beyond the experience and comprehension of soft-living Americans. The Romans conquered their known world more or less with their bare hands through a discipline which terms like "work ethic" do not begin to describe. These republicans routinely committed what we consider atrocious war crimes and crimes against humanity. Jesus was not the only guy they tacked up on a cross. They were known to line both sides of their highways (road building was one of their things, too) with crucified people. Modern Americans share a penchant for capital punishment with the Romans but may draw a line at a Julius Caesar who would go into enemy towns in what is now France, chop off the sword hands of every able bodied man and then write home bragging about it.

Those dreaming of an American empire might ask themselves if they have the moxie for it. The empire business, when viewed from an individual's point of view, is similar to capital punishment. Unless you know you've got what it takes to stick the needles in the veins of the condemned, you shouldn't be arguing for it. To win and run an empire you need a Roman stomach. You need to be able to destroy homes, burn villages, torture captives, shoot hostages, rape women in front of their parents, carry out reprisals on innocents; those kinds of activities. The Republican Romans could do those things, and once upon a time, the monarchical British, the Spanish, and so forth could do likewise. We Americans have also had our little imperial moments, but today, inside the terrarium, acts of that kind are not acceptable.

Ancient Rome is an example of preemptive, aggressive warfare by a democracy, but the contemporary blood and guts party uses the imperial concept to push another, related policy. They have stumbled on the Pax Romana, the two hundred year period after the republic was replaced by autocracy, from the reign of Augustus to that of Marcus Aurelius, when the millions within the empire's boundaries lived in peace. In emulation there is to be a Pax Americana, or a supervision of the globe by the United States under which human kind thrives in amity and free trade. For the Roman army, however, the Pax was more like a pox than a pax. The fighting on the borders of the empire was endless and involved the home team absorbing some costly military defeats. Pax Americana sounds altruistic, idealistic, and laudably boy-scoutish—the generous Americans doing something good again—but it can't be enforced with our atomic-tipped spears, as the frustrating American experience in Iraq should make obvious. Weapons of mass destruction, automated warfare, women soldiers in front of monitors in darkened rooms typing instructions to obedient, electronic bombs will doubtless have a part to play in the upcoming war with China, but for the ordinary work of peace-keeping or nation-building or making the natives behave, it is boots on the ground, as the generals say. Pax Americana will be infantry and military police going to uncomfortable, fly blown, flea bitten, far away places where funny little dyspeptic people take pot shots at them.

Americans do not have Roman mettle. There will be few volunteers.

In the 21st century it seems that Americans talk the talk of military action, but walking the walk is another matter. War movies depicting the heroic battlefield deeds of our grand-parents and ancestors are hits, and occasions for actors and politicians to give speeches which bring tears to the eyes. We can boast of gigantic armies of arcade warriors and combat veterans of Nintendo wars, people who glory in watching the high-IQ munitions demonstrations the Pentagon puts on television. In America the rugged life culture, the kind from which soldiers spring, is confined to watching TV survivor programs. Despite the blather and noisy contention about gun control, every year the number of hunters grows fewer and their median age rises, while the rest of the American population gains weight and shuns the outdoors unless it can be seen through the windows of an air conditioned camper. These fatties, bursting out of their uniforms, will make a nice contrast to the emaciated human forms in some of the very much less developed countries where they will be sent to do their part in maintaining the Pax Americana.

The armed services maintain their manpower levels by making out that they are as much trade schools as military organizations. Even in periods when unemployment is up and jobs are hard to come by, there are no waiting lists for places in the armed services. A hundred years ago many judges gave riffraff convicted of not-too-terrible crimes the choice of the penitentiary or signing up with the peace-time army. With the coming of the Cold War, permanent peace-time conscription was set in place and the services dispensed with the riffraff. Permanent conscription ended in the 1970s when too many draftees were coming home from Vietnam in body bags. The heat was too much for the politicians, who had to end the draft. No soldier boys, no war. As of now the new technologies have ended the era of the *levee en masse* which dominated big-nation warfare from the Napoleonic through the Vietnam War, but for Liberia, Somalia, the Philippines, Peru and, of course, the occupation of Iraq, they have not yet been able to replace troopers with machines. To make the Pax Americana work, this would be the moment to return to the riffraff policy of old. There are more than two million people in the jails and penitentiaries, convicted of the same old, not-too-terrible crimes who might fill up the ranks, but the times will not stand for it, and you cannot trust riffraff with all that expensive, complicated equipment the armed services depends on. It was different back when you could ship them out from the county jail to shovel coal into the boilers of one of Teddy Roosevelt's battleships.

Regardless of that, the Pax Americana crowd want to carry out their ideas by making recalcitrant countries come to heel. They have a list: Saudi Arabia, Syria, and Iran are on it. Since the soldiers needed to fight these wars are not going to be riffraff or any other sort of Americans, they will have to be hired from Poland, from Hungary, maybe even from a few Muslim countries, if they dare. The Romans used rent-a-soldiers, too, and if the Heritage Foundation and the rest who are hell bent on hegemony can channel back to the Romans, somebody from antiquity might get on the line and explain the drawbacks of hiring other people to do your fighting for you. Beside often not doing it well, they have been known to turn on their employers.

And then there was the glory of Greek democracy. They invented the rule of the people as a system of government and gave it its name, but that did not make the democratic city states the less insufferable, piggish and aggressive when they were having the classical equivalent of bad hair days. Athens, the mother of democracy, all but destroyed herself following a plot outline which parallels America's in the last 70 years—at least up to this point, for our drama is not yet played out.

Athens, the democracy, and Sparta, the monarchy, led the other Greek city states in the defense of freedom against the Persians, much as America led the resistance against world communism. After the Persian Wars and the Greek victory over what the history books used to call Oriental despotism, Athens approached its allies with an eye to starting a NATO-like organization called the Delian League. So far so good, but then Athens, full of itself and full of desire for power and wealth, began demanding money and obedience from its fellow league members so persistently that states which began as allies were turned into subdivisions of a new Athenian empire, one which was no less imperial for being democratically based. The upshot was the Peloponnesian Wars, the long struggle between Athens and the Greek states, some of which were democracies themselves, and which would not yield their freedom to the domination of their imperial democratic rival.

In the terrarium such information on democracies, ancient and modern, is widely available and widely unknown. The nation's libraries bulge with books on the subject. Yet people are taught to believe that if democracies have a failing, it is their slowness to sense danger and prepare themselves against looming threats from dictatorships. Other than an endearing optimism which prevents them from taking accurate measure of the present danger, democracies are close to pluperfect. Anyone who says different is a self-hating American.

9.
Hitler

ERHAPS IN EXPIATION FOR his crimes, Adolf has put himself at the service of American war politics. In the biosphere he is the all-purpose cautionary tale. One of the reasons advanced for sending American and British armed forces backpacking into Iraq was the similarity between Saddam Hussein and Hitler. Saddam was a Muslim Hitler who had to be stopped before he. . . . The end of that sentence was left dangling so that hyperthyroid minds could envision the tyrant's battalions of ski-masked terrorists overrunning the world. In actuality Saddam was to Hitler as a snapping turtle is to a saber toothed tiger. That they are both carnivorous is about all they have in common. Be that as it may, the drill is to designate whoever is to be rubbed out as another Hitler.

In the 1980s when Saddam was heavily into mass murder, they were not calling him another Hitler, however. Then he

was an unsightly but useful tool in the conflict which the
United States was carrying on against Iran and the ayatol-
lahs. Years after Saddam had slacked off in the mass murder
department, along comes George Bush, who starts calling
him Hitler, Junior. The explanation for why Saddam had
slacked off is problematic. Had his mullah told him
butchery is un-Islamic? Did he have an attack of conscience? Had he run through his A-list of victims? For
whatever reasons, he was not killing people with the speed,
gusto, or volume in 2003 that he had been twenty years
before, when lives might have been saved by a military
intervention. By the time George W. Bush had the American Army cakewalk into Iraq most of the bodies were
moldering in the ground.

Hitler has other uses besides serving as a rationalization
for knocking off dictators and despots of the second and
third rank. He stands as the paramount example of what
happens when the United States gives in to appeasement.
The homily goes this way: If the democracies had stood up
to Hitler in the early 1930s, there would have been no Holo-
caust, no World War II, ergo any form of negotiation or
accommodation with bad people or disreputable nations is
appeasement and appeasement always leads to the deaths of
the innocent millions. This argument is applied with blind
impartiality to any and every situation. It has even been used
as a justification for refusing to speak with Yasir Arafat as he
sits in his bombed-out headquarters with a crack made by
an Israeli bullet in the only pot he has to pee in. In situation
after situation American foreign policy brutalists start

shouting about gutless softies who still cannot accept that there are a lot of bad guys "out there."

In point of historical fact, the United States did not appease Adolf Hitler or any other dictator in the 1930s. For some years it sat the European crisis out in stone cold neutrality. That appeasement distinction, if there is any, goes to the English and the French, who buckled to Hitler and let him eat up Austria, which was dying to be the Nazis' Linzertorte, and Czechoslovakia, which was not. Doubtless appeasement was one of the major reasons the western democracies let Hitler have his way, but they were not above feeding him a few small tidbit countries in hopes that he would slake his aggressive urges on the Bolsheviks in the Soviet Union. Those kind of carom shots may work in billiards, but in international politics, the ball has a way of popping off the table.

When the CIA trained and armed those earnest young Muslim freedom fighters to kick the Soviets out of Afghanistan in the 1980s, they did not imagine in their wildest nightmares that they were playing a major role in the creation of al Qaeda. Similarly, when the major democracies, the United States included, assisted Saddam in his invasion of and war against Iran in the 1980s no one could foresee that what they were doing would lead to Iraq's invasion of Kuwait in 1991 and the gooey mess from which the United States has yet to extricate itself.

Hitler is a valuable assistant in the selling of a new and always expensive weapon. The line runs like this: Democracies are slow to arm themselves for their own defense because democracies are such sleepy, trusting, good-intentioned nations. The proof of this statement is that democracies failed to arm themselves while Hitler was building the most powerful army in the world. And, indeed, that may have been the case with Britain and France in the 1930s, a reaction to the slaughter begun in 1914 when they were armed to the teeth. However, in America, President Franklin Roosevelt did his level best to arm the nation, though Congress was not similarly disposed. In general, democracies have managed to defend themselves quite adequately. If that were not the case there would be no democracies to write about.

10

Conversation Stiflers

FLOATING THROUGH THE ATMOSPHERE of the terrarium are dogmatic dust mites or shibboleths which, when exhaled into the other person's face, end debate and discussion. After getting a whiff of these standbys, the recipient sits down and shuts up. No rejoinder is permissible after you have been reminded that "Politics stops at the water's edge," meaning you may not dispute foreign policy.

Politics does not stop at the water's edge or any place else. Politics is everywhere, and whenever you hear somebody talking about a non-political endeavor you may be sure that you are listening to a liar or an idiot. What stops at the water's edge in a war-or-peace discussion is political courage. If you persist in your objections, you will be accused of being unpatriotic. Try and wiggle out of that one. Thus the water's edge is a tool of intimidation, not a description of fact; as such, it works well.

"I support our young men and women over there in harm's way," says the speaker, who means, "I hate this damnable war but I'm afraid to say so." Opposing wars in the United States can end a career. Americans like to go to war, or at least they do not object to going, either because the United States has always been on the right side, or they associate war with good stuff like prosperity, or they are not that interested. In 225 years of war only once can it be said that an anti-war or peace movement in America had any success. That was during the Vietnam War, but even then the peace movement only got real traction after the conflict had been going on for years, literally almost as long as the Second World War. There are no instances of an American peace movement having prevented a war.

"The United States will not enter into discussions with bad men or wicked governments," and its variant, "We will only talk to responsible leaders of other countries," takes us on a short hop, skip, and jump to telling another country to get rid of their dictator, president, or prime minister and choose a leader we like. There are few faster ways to end negotiations. The Bush people tried this approach on the North Koreans and had to back down.

One way to make sure you have a responsible and worthy foreign leader to deal with is to put him in office yourself. In the 1980s the Americans and Israelis did something of that sort in Lebanon. A Maronite Christian general, Amin Gemayal, was made president of that distressed and then nearly destroyed country. Accommodating fellow that he was, Gemayal signed a treaty with the Israelis. All went well until his fellow countrymen found out what was in the treaty. Years of fighting and killing followed and did not end until the Israelis were driven out of Lebanon. The Soviets in Afghanistan made a similar move, installing a chap named Muhammad Najibullah as the head of government. In due course Mr. Najibullah could be seen at the end of a noose dangling from a Taliban gibbet.

Even semi-acceptables like Hosni Mubarak of Egypt and the various heads of government in Pakistan, Morocco and Saudi Arabia, whom the United States did not pick but whom it blesses and backs, live their lives in the cross-hairs of the assassin's rifle. The number of heads of government and other officials from those countries who have been murdered by their own countrymen over the last 20 or 30 years should give pause to anyone who thinks that if you can slip the right person in at the top, good things will follow.

If it were not self evident, Machiavelli would have laid down a rule saying that you do not get to pick the boss of the other side. You do not even want to pick the other side's boss, because he will not be able to carry out the bargain you strike with him for the simple reason that he will have no support among his own people. To the Americans he is a responsible leader, to his people he is a Quisling.

For a quarter of a century the Americans and the Israelis have been looking to replace Yasir Arafat, surely a less than loveable character, with an acceptable (to them) substitute. He is not, we were told, a "suitable partner for peace." But that is so much tail chasing. The only suitable partner for peace is he who can make a deal and make it stick. Slobodan Milosovic did that in Yugoslavia. Mass murderer or not, he made the deal and the guns fell silent.

The ultimate trump card for those wanting to wash out the opposition is to call on the American People.

> "The polls say that the American People will pay any price to strip Saddam of his weapons of mass destruction."
>
> "By three to one the American People believe Saddam has weapons of mass destruction and will use them on Philadelphia."

Case closed. You cannot beat the American People when they give judgment via a public opinion survey, though you can counter by educing a poll of your own saying the opposite. Sometimes that works, but the red, white, and bluest poll is usually the one which wins. If you've got the guts, you can say that the American People are wrong and get yourself tabbed as an elitist. You can say, if you dare, that the American People are asses, dolts, and blockheads, but the penalties for political snobbism are severe. You will be judged according to a western version of *sharia*, the Islamic code of law, found guilty and stoned to death like an adulterous woman in Mecca.

"We seek not one inch of territory for ourselves, therefore we are pure of heart and without base motives or hidden agendas, and thus entitled to invade your country." This and similar statements may work on one's fellow Americans, but Europeans and Fijians are rarely won over. George Bush used this approach when he announced he was off on his invasion: "We have no ambition in Iraq, except to remove a threat and restore control of that country to its own people." Self-serving statements about morals and motives which, outside the terrarium, are heard with astonishment and disbelief are accepted in the biosphere for gospel truth.

11

Tassels on the Fringe

NDER THE DOME WHICH shelters America from the real reality, a public figure who has not been called a racist, a homophobe, an anti-Semite, a nut job, a Communist or a bigot of some description is probably a scoundrel. Still, there are certain topics which, when raised, guarantee that the speaker will be called nasty names and shown the exit at the next election.

The closet-liberal members of Congress from the Southern states kept their mouths shut for years. They voted against civil rights legislation, backed filibusters and even forced themselves to makes speeches and sign declarations whose meanings made some of them wish to vomit. They convinced themselves that, though they held on to their places by lying and misrepresentation, the nation was better off with them than those who would take their seats in Congress, were they to tell the voters their true beliefs.

Nowadays the voters' position on civil rights has changed
and a politician risks getting chucked out of office if he or
she fails to show up for the Martin Luther King Jr. Day cel-
ebrations. It is other topics which can end a public career.
Though Social Security has been called the third rail of
American politics, it is low voltage compared to deviating
from the party line on the Middle East.

As far back as the 1980s, 11-term Republican Congressman
Paul Findley and Charles Percy, chairman of the Senate Foreign Relations Committee, earned themselves early retire-
ment from elective politics for minor acts of deviation from
the submissive party line on the State of Israel. Both Findley
and Percy, a three-term Senator whose heresies on the question were quite mild, lost in close elections after their oppo-
nents got significant material assistance from pro-Israeli
activists. Debate on Israel is an impermissible subject under
the dome, although elsewhere in the world, including in
Israel itself, policy disputes about who did what right and
who did it wrong and what should be done next can be carried on without worrying that your next word will be the last
which will be accorded serious attention.

Findley was defeated in his bid for a 12th term by a combination of redistricting and the American Israel Public
Affairs Committee, or AIPAC, an acronym which strikes
fear in the hearts of Washington politicians who are desperate for campaign money and fearful that AIPAC may,
instead, give the money to their rivals. Findley was so
scarred by what happened to him that he has written five
books on the general subject of Israeli politics and has made

a career of propagating heterodox opinions. This has not made him one of the respected experts to be seen on the PBS nightly news show or featured on CNN with the semi-retired generals and the pro-war think tanks. It has made him a shadow person in the political life of the dome. Findley is someone you can find if you look, but few do.

Misspeak on the Middle East and you become a tassel on the fringe of public life, an extremist, an anti-Semite. The following from the *Washington Post* in the winter of 2003 shows how saying the wrong thing makes a politician a non-person: "Jewish organizations condemned Rep. James P. Moran Jr. (D-Va.) yesterday for delivering what they said were anti-Semitic remarks at an antiwar forum in Reston . . .

"At the forum, attended by about 120 people at St. Anne's Episcopal Church on March 3, Moran discussed why he thought antiwar sentiment was not more effective in the United States.

" 'If it were not for the strong support of the Jewish community for this war with Iraq, we would not be doing this,' Moran said, '. . . The leaders of the Jewish community are influential enough that they could change the direction of where this is going, and I think they should.'

"Moran, a seven-term incumbent representing Alexandria, Arlington County and part of Fairfax County, yesterday apologized in a statement, saying, 'I made some insensitive remarks that I deeply regret.' "

Moran's apologies did him no good. He was stripped of his position as regional minority whip in the House of Representatives, threatened with opposition in the next

Democratic primary and roundly denounced by rabbis and other important Jewish and non-Jewish figures. Threats of the kind aimed at Moran are not to be taken lightly. The American Israel Public Affairs Committee, a lobbying and political money organization with a reputation as being at least as dangerous and/or helpful as the fabled American Association of Retired People (AARP), can crush a politician with the same crinkly sound and authority as a heel on a cockroach. Hence the slobbering, undignified apology of a man forced to take back words which he believes to be true.

If James Moran is not an anti-Semite, there are anti-Semites under the dome, but nobody can say how many. The Anti-Defamation League (ADL), which counts overt anti-Semitic acts, reports that they are occurring at the rate of about fifteen hundred a year and are markedly up on college campuses. That anti-Semitism is more prevalent than it has been is the opinion of Harvard University President Lawrence H. Summers who says of himself, "I am Jewish, identified but hardly devout." Last September he told an audience in Memorial Church, Cambridge, Massachusetts, "Where anti-Semitism and views that are profoundly anti-Israeli have traditionally been the primary preserve of poorly educated right-wing populists, profoundly anti-Israel views are increasingly finding support in progressive intellectual communities. Serious and thoughtful people are advocating and taking actions that are anti-Semitic in their effect if not their intent." A major definition shift here. You can be guilty of something without doing the thing or intending to do the thing. You can be an unintentional anti-Semite, meaning you can harbor no ill will or prejudice toward Jewish people and still be an anti-Semite. Once upon a time in the turgid, ingrown language of the Communist Party some people were labeled "premature anti-fascist" or Hitler haters during the (1939–1941) period of the Nazi-Communist alliance, when the party line was that Hitler was an okay kind of guy. Unintentional anti-Semitism has the same ring to it, a dictum or *fatwa* or rescript handed down from headquarters to be adhered to but not discussed.

Summers has got hold of something here. There has been a shifting of opinion. Seemingly "poorly educated right-wing populists," or Christian fanatics, have moved over to being, if not pro-Jewish, then pro-Israel at the same time as members of "progressive intellectual communities" have become, if not anti-Jewish, then anti-Israel. Mr. Summers takes note of the super WASP denominations, i.e., Anglicans, Lutherans, Presbyterians, Methodists, Disciples et al, who appear to be gradually dying out even as their sympathies have become pronouncedly pro-Palestinian. Something of the same has happened in the African-American world, which 50 years ago was staunchly in the Israeli corner but now faces in the other direction.

In his church address Summers gave examples of current "actions that are anti-Semitic in their effect if not their intent." They are:

"Hundreds of European academics have called for an end to support for Israeli researchers, though not for an end to support for researchers from any other nation.

"Israeli scholars this past spring were forced off the board of an international literature journal.

"At the same rallies where protesters, many of them university students, condemn the IMF and global capitalism and raise questions about globalization, it is becoming increasingly common to also lash out at Israel. Indeed, at the anti-IMF rallies last spring, chants were heard equating Hitler and Sharon.

"Events to raise funds for organizations of questionable political provenance that in some cases were later found to support terrorism have been held by student organizations on this and other campuses with at least modest success and very little criticism.

"And some here at Harvard and some at universities across the country have called for the University to single out Israel among all nations as the lone country where it is inappropriate for any part of the university's endowment to be invested. I hasten to say the University has categorically rejected this suggestion."

In his choice of examples Summers comes close to saying that attacking Israel is the same as being anti-Semitic. On this point he says, "I have always throughout my life been put off by those who heard the sound of breaking glass, in every insult or slight, and conjured up images of Hitler's Kristallnacht at any disagreement with Israel. Such views have always seemed to me alarmist if not slightly hysterical. But I have to say that while they still seem to me unwarranted, they seem rather less alarmist in the world of today than they did a year ago." That sounds as if two or three more negative opinions about Israel are tantamount to adjudging the speaker an anti-Semite. Summers comes close to saying it; others hold the position outright.

Nobody knows how many anti-Semites there are in America, of the real kind or of the unintentional Lawrence Summers' kind. With something like this there is no way of guessing the percentages. We can count the number of Summers' "serious and thoughtful" persons in "progressive intellectual communities" who are categorized as haters by the Harvard president because they talk like "poorly educated right-wing populists." There cannot be too many of them, however. They are a *rara avis* by his own definition.

There is another type of *avis* which may not be so *rara,* even if sociological bird watchers may have trouble counting them. These are people who keep their own council on the subject of Israel and the Middle East. There must be a bunch of them in those "progressive intellectual communities" where the boss can deny you promotion and tenure if it turns out you are an unintentional anti-Semite. To them we can add those outside the progressive, intellectual communities who have decided for social and business reasons that the prudent thing to do is to keep their mouths zippered. They often are literate, college educated managers and professionals. They do not want to be screamed at by intemperate zealots at dinner parties, or denounced for holding opinions they do not hold and which are repugnant to them. Reticence is safer and easier, especially if their only connection to the Middle East is ownership of a low miles per gallon automobile. It may only be dawning on them now that the American Israeli policy is, step by step, taking the nation into a world of pain, but what is the point of saying anything? The next thing you know somebody will be telling people that you are soft on terrorism.

When the poll takers come around, respondents are not going to tell them what they really think on such topics any more than they will tell anybody else whom they don't know or don't have reason to trust. Hence, there is no telling if we are dealing with one half of one percent of the population or two percent or what. Moreover, persons like Lawrence Summers are muddying the waters by broadening the definition of anti-Semitism to include people whose politics he does not like but who are indifferent or positive in their thinking about Jewish people and the Jewish religion. We don't know, but I'll hazard a guess they are more numerous and more significant and less visible than those people figuring in Summers' examples.

The feeling of being gagged and intimidated is apparently growing and, with it, a resentment which has a nasty edge. People taking Summers' position, that is, vociferously pro-Israel, can have little sense of the existence of a large number of discreet individuals who hold opinions diametrically opposite to his own, although, since they seem to be all over, a person such as Summers probably deals with some of them every day in his own office. They will keep their traps shut and tell him not what they think, but what they know he wants to think that they think. Some of those people dissembling in front of him may also be Jewish. It is not only non-Jews who take discretion over valor and keep their opinions to themselves when it comes to dangerous topics.

Since 9/11 it seems that the number of silent dissenters has markedly increased and since the Iraqi invasion they have been joined by more subterranean grumblers. The secret resentment and anger is not unlike an underground peat fire. You know it's there but how deep it smolders and how long and how hot it may burn, no one can say.

Foreigners pressing their noses against the glass panes of the American greenhouse cannot see the code word/coal mine political life going on underneath the surface. In broad daylight above ground, people lie, dissemble and keep quiet; below, in the darkness, people meet, probe each other to make sure that they have found a kindred spirit, and then say what they actually think. Muslims, too, one supposes, are down in the tunnels. Are there mosques where conspirators meet? The bombs are real, the people at the World Trade Center are dead. A price is being paid for those things we don't discuss.

In the land of the free and the home of the timid and intimidated, the President goes to war for reasons he cannot explain and it is better to let him do it than truncate your future by arguing. In the misty life of the biosphere, protesting has become something akin to a monastic vocation. Once you do it, you find you have crossed a line and become a tassel on the political fringe. You run the risk of being referred to as an activist or even a militant, which is but a few degrees south of crackpot.

The American custom is to forgive a person one protest.

After that you must live a blameless political life within the confines of the two-party system. A second protest and you are a -winger, left or right, but whichever side of the bird you are assigned, your goose is cooked. You become like Ramsey Clark, United States Attorney General in the Lyndon Johnson administration, now condemned to wander the earth as a mendicant friar, begging justice in mostly lost causes.

12

They Lie . . . Sometimes

THE PEOPLE OF THE crystal dome have been known to become agitated when it is revealed to them that their government has not told them the truth. They soon forget, which makes it possible for them to be surprised, upset, and angry when it happens again. America is quite an old country, already well into its third century, and by now its people have been lied to more times than a month of TV commercials, but they still get upset at being told untruths by those whom they have elected. This is said to be a sign of the nation's enduring idealism and high ethical standards. That may be so, or it may be a sign of political infantilism, a refusal to recognize that one has grown up and been allotted a place in the adult world of nations.

The nation which invented the lap dance still thinks of itself as young, pure, and virginal. Outside the great crystal palace people from other cultures and other climes have a decidedly different take on the American insistence on its innocence. When the wise old heads on television sadly pronounce once again that, "America has lost its innocence," they wonder if such persistent naivety isn't innocence but stupidity. He who forgets the last lie is more open to believing the next.

From the Spanish-American War forward there have been an unending series of official cock and bull stories which have been taken as sober fact by the public. Some of the stories were so obviously unbelievable that the masses had to be complicitous in their own deception. The idea that the enfeebled Spanish government, collapsing in imperial desuetude, would for no reason blow up the battleship Maine as it visited one of its ports is self-evident trash, but highly serviceable for starting the 1898 Spanish-American War.

World War I propaganda about Prussian Schrecklichkeit or terrorism based itself on countless, fictitious stories of murder, plunder and rape. The American imagination was, from 1916 to 1918, littered with women dishonored and babies bayoneted by the slobbering Hun. The following text was written for a poster aimed at under draft-age college boys to get them warmed up and ready when their time in the trenches came: "In the vicious gutteral [sic] language of Kultur, the degree A. B. means bachelor of atrocities. Are you going to let the Prussian Python strike at your Alma Mater . . . ? The Hohenzollern fang strikes at every element of decency and culture and taste that your college stands for." Any similarity in this form of speech with what may be heard any night on cable television must be coincidental because, while the World War I propaganda was false, what greets the eyes and ears now vis-a-vis Arabs, Muslims, and such like is surely true; it is an article of faith among the inhabitants of the biosphere that material progress has been matched by a concomitant growth in goodness.

In the 1930s a certain number of Americans fought free of amnesia and remembered what they had been told by their betters about Germany in the months leading up to World War I. When similar stories about the Nazis began coming out of Germany twenty years later, they did not believe. Fool me once, your fault; fool me twice, mine. Some of these people supported the America First isolationist movement, which opposed involvement in the European war. In general, however, lying does work. If it didn't, fewer politicians would do it; although as the Bush-Iraq fiasco demonstrates, some artfulness, some talent and intelligence is needed.

Lying and/or withholding the facts—which is much the same thing—is often done for the public's good. When the Japanese air force sank or severely damaged all the battleships of the United States' Pacific Fleet, Americans were not told about it. Not only didn't American officials admit what had happened, they told reporters that ships which were resting on the bottom of the sea at Pearl Harbor were still afloat. The Japanese had planes zipping over the American naval base; they knew what they had sunk. They could see it. The lying was strictly for home consumption.

Officials also played down the fact that during the 1930s America was supplying Japan with the materiel for its armed forces. Though not prominent in the newspapers, it was a common, if bitter, belief in New York that when the 6th Avenue "El" was torn down the scrap was sold to Japan—which returned it in the form of bullets and bombs. The selling of arms to putative enemies predates Iraq by a millennium or two.

How the people in government thought they could get away with some of their whoppers is past imagining. After the atomic bomb was dropped on Hiroshima, talk started getting around that there were post-bomb deaths caused by radiation. The government immediately denied it and the head of the Manhattan Project, Major General Leslie R. Groves, pronounced that, "This talk about radio-activity is so much nonsense." What was the point of that one? And how long did they think they could get away with it? So much high level lying is purposeless, done from habit. How else to explain the line of half-baked, nutty, next-day-refutable lies coming out of the Bush White House about weapons, terrorists, plans, and intentions?

American prisoners being returned by the North Koreans after the cease-fire ended hostilities in 1953 were ordered to sign statements promising not to discuss anything having to do with captivity to any media representative not bound by Pentagon censorship rules. Washington did not want the country to know about the degree and kind of collaboration with the enemy which took place in the prison camps.

The peccadilloes of the Korean War have been lost in the continuing miasma about the truths and the falsities of the Vietnam War. Long book shelves are devoted to volumes

discussing lies told, lies exposed, and lies retold in connection with that war, whose shadow falls obliquely on George
Bush's Dance in the Desert almost forty years later.

Officially, the full Vietnam War began with events in the
Gulf of Tonkin, August 1 and 4, 1964, when, according to
the American government, a couple of North Vietnamese
patrol boats attacked a U.S. destroyer.

This was the lie upon which Congress voted, with only
two nay votes in the Senate and none in the House, what
amounted to a declaration of war. But was the report of the
action in the Tonkin Gulf a lie? And if it was a lie, what kind
of a lie? To this day there is considerable doubt that a
second attack ever occurred, but what of the first? Whatever
kind of attack it was, the destroyer survived unscathed and
probably untouched by the arrows, spears, and whatever
else a tiny patrol boat could launch at a mighty modern
cruiser.

The nation and its editorial pages launched their own
attacks against the North Vietnamese, as every institution of
authority and prestige, and all major media, including the
Washington Post and the *New York Times,* cheered the
oncoming war, which would eventually see a half a million
American troops engaged—of whom more than ten percent
would come back dead. Later on many who could not wait
to get on with the war would say they had been lied to and
that, if they had known the truth, they would never have
supported sending the boys over there. And thereby may
hang the real lie, and the biggest one of all.

Americans seem to look on life in their terrarium as a

Garden of Eden before the serpent showed up and did a traveling salesman routine on the lady of the household. There is not supposed to be any crying in baseball and there is not supposed to be any lying by the government in the Garden of Eden. In the Edenic paradise they tell us the truth and we believe them and act accordingly. But they don't tell the truth, and if the game that is played under the dome is to pretend that they do, it is a dangerous game.

Knowing a little of the history of lying mitigates against this form of self-delusion. If a person studies history for a short while, it will come to the person that the government lies a lot, maybe even all the time. If you know that they lie, you may be able to see that the lie of the hour is farcical and far fetched; you know to disbelieve it. That should have been the case with the Tonkin Gulf attack in the summer of 1964 which, true or false, was by the government's own description little more than a bunch of guys in a dugout canoe paddling out into the Pacific Ocean to attack the picket boats of a mighty armada with blowpipes or some other instrument with equivalent capacity to inflict damage on a modern ship o' war. People believed this lie, if it was a lie, or made much of this ridiculous little incident, if it was not a lie, because, willy-nilly, like Hitler and Poland, the people who bought the story were aching to go to war. Like 1939, one side was itching for war and would use any pretext, no matter how small, to start one. Hitler made one up out of whole cloth; the Americans may or may not have made one up, but the incident they chose to use as provocation for a war which caused the deaths of hundreds of thousands was a whiffling moment whose importance was vastly out of proportion to whatever may have occurred.

When, on December 29, 1989, with little public notice, more than 20,000 American soldiers invaded Panama, the reason given was the capture of the country's drug pusher–CIA operative–dictator–and–bully boy Manuel Noriega. The actual reasons are subject to speculation to this day. The invasion may have been to make Panamanians understand that the independence the United States had recently granted them and their canal was for show only. Or it may have been that Noriega, a dirt bag if there ever was one, had been party to deals with the American government and the administration of Bush the elder was afraid he'd try his hand at blackmail. Noriega was taken off to Florida, where he got a taste of American courtroom justice and was thrown into a dungeon, where he resides as of this writing.

The events in and around the Panama invasion are open to the vilest interpretations because the only reporters the government allowed were literally kept locked up in a warehouse until the fun was over. The festivities included the deaths of 2,000 and the wounding of perhaps 70,000 Panamanians, as well as the burning of parts of their capital city. Although a few malcontents have brought the Panama episode up from time to time, overall the government's lying by silence and secrecy seems to have worked well for the people in charge.

A *coup de main* brought off by a brigade or two of soldiers, and even perhaps the unexplained deaths, could be done by lying through stealth and censorship, but Gulf War

I was too big to be done without somebody saying something, true or untrue. You would have thought that Saddam
Hussein's indefensible invasion of Kuwait was enough, but,
à la World War I, the western ministries of truth had to gild
the lily, updating the old Hun atrocity stories about killing
babies, etc. Why did they make up tales of atrocities about
Saddam when there were bucketfuls of authenticated stories
about his murders, rapes, tortures and thefts? It is almost as
if the government liars wished to discredit themselves and
their cause.

They also made overreaching claims concerning the
ability of the United States Air Force to perform "surgical
strikes," which all but eliminated civilian casualties unless
Saddam was using them as hostages (as if killing a few civilians ever stopped any army anywhere or anytime). This prevarication got the military involved in a succession of
controversies each time one of its bombs went awry and
killed "innocent" civilians. (Parenthetically, are there any
other kind of civilians, and is one justified, if there are, in
killing "guilty" ones, or is the term one more cliché of the
propagandist's craft? Its use, which is almost universal, is a
sure clue the speaker is selling a point of view.)

You would think that in a war easily won against an all
but impotent opponent, the winning side might want to
pick up credit by scrupulously telling the truth. Losers are
always liars, but why should winners be the same? Commanding General Norman Schwarzkopf told the press that,
"The Patriot's success, of course, is known to everyone. It's
one hundred percent." President Bush, the elder, said much

the same thing, when the military knew perfectly well this missile could not hit the broad side of a barn on a sunny day. These lies were probably not primarily aimed at the inhabitants of the biosphere but at Israeli citizens. The United States did not want Israel in the war for fear it would rile up its Arab allies, but Saddam was hurling his own inaccurate, but nevertheless frightening, missiles at Israel. Since it would take a few days to shut the Iraqis down, it was decided to lie to the Israelis, who were to think they were protected when they were not.

That kind of lying works. It is a political version of the placebo effect. If a trustworthy and respected source says something false, it will be taken for true even against the evidence of one's eyes and ears. They would not lie if people did not believe the lies, and to make acceptance more likely, about half of what they say is true. But there is no easy method for figuring out which half.

The pattern repeats itself in Iraq. If you wanted to go to war regardless of the excuse, or if you didn't care particularly or weren't interested in politics or you accepted whatever your betters told you, then you took the shoddy stuff that Bush, Cheney, Powell, Wolfowitz, and Rumsfeld were pumping out with no questions asked. All the newspapers and television stations echoed back at the boss politicians, "Good to go!", and from one end of the vast crystalline biosphere to the other, the cry went up, "Ready to rumble, red, white, and blue!"

13

War Whores

"If they'd show the head wounds, there wouldn't be war"
—an elderly pacifist woman.

OOK, IN THE HISTORY of television news, anybody who's anybody has some sort of combat experience. You look at the giants, you look at a Rather, you look at a Peter Jennings . . . These are guys who all made their reputations covering war . . . It's clear to anybody who is trying to make a career for one's self what war can mean," quoth Jim Axelrod of CBS, who understands that the oil companies and munitions makers are not the only ones who have a material interest in the shooting.

The ambitious Mr. Axelrod is not the first to make a name for himself covering a war, no more than his giants are. The great age for war reporting began somewhere around the time of the Civil War, when editors started to print the bylines of the men writing the battlefield dispatches rather than the anonymous "from our correspondent." They were gifted and ballsy men—and they were mostly men—and included in their roster such names as Winston Churchill and Stephen Crane, who took up the calling after he had written *The Red Badge of Courage* and before he had ever been in the remote vicinity of a shot fired in anger.

From the 1890s through the start of World War I the most famous American war correspondent was Richard Harding Davis (1864–1916), a man of considerable talent at both dramatizing himself and writing. Some people give him credit for inventing personal journalism in the modern sense and for having influenced the style of a string of writers ranging down through the decades from Frank Norris and Ernest Hemingway to Norman Mailer. Correspondents in Davis' time did not necessarily see themselves as neutrals and were known to pick up a gun when the occasion called for it. Davis went up San Juan Hill with Teddy Roosevelt in the capacity of a journalist and a combatant. If they did not play by modern rules, journalists of Davis' stripe had their ideas of right and wrong. Although it cost the Anglophile Davis membership in his London club, during the Boer War Davis left off covering the war from the British perspective and switched sides, writing that, "As I see it, it has been a Holy War, this Burgher Crusade, and their motives are as fine as any that called a 'minute man' from his farm, or sent a Knight of the Cross to die for it in Palestine."

In the course of Gulf War I the performing seals of television news became known as "scud studs" because what they lacked in ability and judgment, they compensated for as eye candy. (The scud was an inaccurate Soviet missile used by Saddam.) These young people brought to the coverage of war a certain lubricious quality not previously present in this branch of journalism. They were not unlike the camp followers who have constituted the tail of armies since the time of Xerxes, the ancient Persian emperor.

The name "war whore" is better suited to them. They are the ladies and gentlemen of the media who whooped, hollered and thigh-slapped the United States into and through Gulf II. Day in and day out, hour after hour, on the TV cable news channels especially, they tingled with happy excitement as they strained to infect viewers (and less often, readers) with the upside of death and disfigurement.

However much war may depress advertising and ruin the news budgets of the big media corporations, it gooses the ratings and it makes stars of the on-air performers—and heroes, too. As the war grew close to starting, HBO showed *Live from Baghdad,* a docudrama glamorizing war whoredom. The true-to-life version of the show was available around the clock as the war whores promoted themselves and their careers in real time on their TV channels. Their glistening eyes, their happily agitated voices, their perturbed, gulping deliveries, their stagy bathos added to the erotic energy they invested in their talk of freedom, courage and victory over the non-resisting foe.

The Pentagon did a one-eighty from Gulf I to Gulf II in handling the media. Instead of keeping the reporters back and away from the action, the two and a half thousand of them who turned up to cover the walk-over which was called a war were invited to be "embedded," or to be the guests of military units of all and every description. The arrangement was much criticized by people who thought that "embedded" meant the same as "co-opted," which it does, but what can you expect? During the Second World War General Eisenhower referred to war correspondents as "assimilated officers" or "quasi–staff officers." The armed services are not going to tolerate obnoxious neutral personalities floating around in their midst, even if it were psychologically possible for the correspondents to keep themselves emotionally separated from the men and women they were living with.

War whores and respectable workaday reporters alike take the side of the army they are with, as John Steinbeck understood when, looking back on his stint as a war correspondent in World War II, he wrote, "We were all part of the war effort. We went along with it, and not only that, we abetted it. Gradually it became a part of us that the truth about anything was automatically secret and that to trifle with it was to interfere with the war effort. By this I don't mean that the correspondents were liars. They were not . . . It is in the things not mentioned that the untruth lies . . . Yes, we wrote only a part of the war but at the time we believed, fervently believed, that it was the best thing to do. And perhaps that is why, when the war was over, novels and stories by ex-soldiers, like *The Naked and the Dead,* proved so shocking to the public which had been carefully protected from contact with the crazy, hysterical mess."

After the conclusion of what passed as hostilities in Iraq, John Burns, the *New York Times*' top man in Baghdad, threw a moral hissy fit because reporters from other organizations were not sufficiently anti-Saddam. They did not do all they might have to back the war effort by exposing Saddam's crimes. "I was the most closely watched and unfavored of all the correspondents there because I wrote about terror whilst Saddam Hussein was still in power," Burns said. "I described how Saddam turned this country into a slaughterhouse . . . I felt that that was central truth that had to be told about this place. It was also the essential truth that was untold by the vast majority of correspondents here. Why? Because they judged that the only way they could keep themselves in play here was to pretend that it was okay . . . Some of my rivals who had omitted to notice that Iraq was a terror state were busy here sucking up." Burns tells of American television suppressing accounts of Saddam's torture chambers and mass murders. He denounces television networks' paying Iraqi officials hundreds of thousands of dollars in bribes to make sure they were not thrown out of the country. How much of Burns' fury is based on an accurate assessment of what the competition did, how much is resentment of rivals, and how much is *Times*-o-centric egotism is for another discussion, but it is certain that with or without the contribution of Burns' rivals, there had been no lack of publicity about Saddam's murders, torture, and cruelties since 1990. Before that, Saddam had his uses in the eyes of the American government, and concomitantly less was said about his butcheries.

Steinbeck's observation that, "It is in the things not mentioned that the untruth lies," raises the question of what a man like Burns, a man on a mission, did not say and may not have noticed. Why, relative to Saddam's crimes, was so little attention paid to the desperate state of the Iraqi infrastructure? What is the connection between the country's advanced dilapidation and its capacity to fight a war? What would have been the reaction had it been widely publicized that, before the Americans waltzed in, there was no electricity half the time, sewer and water systems were on the fritz, industry had almost ceased to function, and large segments of the population were sick and near prostrate because of poor nutrition? If it had been generally understood that Iraq's level of life, technology, and wealth had sunk to something close to Zimbabwe's, how would people have received assertions that Iraq could let fly with missiles of mass destruction forty-five minutes after the order to fire was given?

In general, what did the embeddeds and the unembeddeds, who were given the odd sounding name of unilaterals, see? They had the ability to feel and dwell on experience, but where were their heads, their brains? The press, electronic, digital and Gutenbergian, were slap-happy for human interest, how-did-it-feel stories. The war must be personalized, brought down to the human level. "After I returned to America, I wrote a column saying, 'I'm back,' but I talked to some of the marines who had come back and there was this feeling of missing the war," said Gordon Dillow of the *Orange County Register*, who has the hang of what the editors want. "It was miserable and dirty and uncomfortable and painful and scary and yet there's the feeling that you're doing something that's important, that it's part of history and separate from what everybody else back home is experiencing. You're seeing something that very few people get to see or want to see or will ever have an opportunity to see. There's a rush to that."

The rush was not blood to the brain apparently. The reporters did not see and it did not occur to them that there was no war. Convention holds that a war demands two armies in some form of organized combat, be it ever so brief. What the reporters were involved in was a Boy Scout jamboree during which hostile persons, mounted on Bactrians or riding with grenade launchers in the back of pickup trucks, would, from time to time, hurl their darts at the Humvees in which the chem suit–clad Americans rode in extreme discomfort. This is not a war. To the correspondents who had covered Bosnia or Kosovo and knew of war, it should have been obvious that there was no army in Iraq other than the American one, which was zooming through the desert more or less unopposed. The reporters who had read books describing war and "the crunch of the enemy's artillery" might have noted that no such crunches were to be heard, an observation which in its turn might have led to the thought that, whatever else they were involved in, it was not a war. The mathematically gifted among the journalists should have noticed there were more traffic fatalities than lives lost in combat—a sign to drive slower and tone down the copy. General Custer lost more men to Chief Sitting Bull at the Little Big Horn than the United States lost in the Iraqi "war." (What happened to the Americans in the months after the bowlegged Bush stood on the aircraft carrier and pronounced his war over is a different story. That was war, but one ill-suited for heavy equipment and the death-from-the-sky, kill-quick-and-clean technology which the Americans think of as an artifact of an advanced civilization.)

Back home under the dome the generals and politicians lengthened their strides and set their jaws tighter as befits heroes and leaders, while the media outdid itself in praise of history's greatest war machine. In the list of one-sided conflicts, the American victory in Iraq was right up there at the top with Mussolini's conquest of Ethiopia in 1936 or Stalin's flattening Latvia in 1939. The red, white, and blue yahoos in the media and out of it hailed this passage of arms as the last step in America's recovery from the Vietnam Syndrome, a white liver disease which had afflicted the nation since the peaceniks, the Reds, and the cowards had betrayed the army in the field and forced the United States to agree to a shameful peace. Until Vietnam, America was the country which liked to say that it had never lost a war (Korea was called a tie ball game), but now Uncle Sam was back and he was big. Even Bill Clinton's confused and ignominious withdrawal from Somalia after a brief firefight in Mogadishu was rewritten into another stanza in the Marine anthem when Hollywood gave the country *Blackhawk Down.*

Whether the rah-rah stuff was lying, or making the best of an ambiguous situation, or acknowledging a mighty moment of freedom depends on what you are wearing on your lapel, but in sum it was the old lesson repeated: They may or may not lie to you, but they don't tell you the truth, not all of it, not in a way that lets you get a handle on what's going on. Nevertheless, the raw material for finding out what is happening is in abundant supply. Even now, a time of corporate media octopuses, there is no dearth of information available if people are willing to dig it out and then puzzle it out for themselves.

Pouting because others have not pureed the informational food necessary for thought and sulking because others have failed to honestly, fairly and truthfully do the thinking for people distracted by refinancing their homes is a form of political infantilism not indulged in outside the American demisphere. In other countries grownups know that the truth teat does not exist and, if it did, they wouldn't get to suck on it anyway because the government would have it locked up somewhere.

After the official war was over and the body bags and casualties continued to dribble back from Iraq to Dover Air Force Base in Maryland, a grumbling could be heard here and there across the biosphere. The people, or at least some of the people, were complaining that they had been jobbed.

Americans have a notion that if there is a Food and Drug Administration to guarantee the purity of what they put in their mouths, a similar mechanism ensures the purity of what goes into their brains. It's easier to believe that than to dope it out for themselves, taken up as they are with more important things than war and peace, like pro football and self improvement. After the fact, after it has begun to dawn on them that they have been had, they phone the call-in programs or vote on the Internet or gripe to whoever will listen to them about media bias. But under the vast crystal curve, the reason the war whores prosper is because the people are their johns.

14.
Missionaries

BATTLE HYMN OF THE REPUBLIC REVISED
Mine eyes have seen the launching of
the orgy of the Sword;
He is searching out the hoardings where
the strangers' wealth is stored;
He hath loosed his fateful lightnings,
and with woe and death has scored;
His lust is marching on.
—Mark Twain, 1900

I N 1805 CHRISTIAN FUNDAMENTALIST missionaries met with chiefs and braves from the Six Nations near Buffalo Creek, New York, where the clergy people behaved as the Jerry Falwells and Billy Grahams are wont to do. A response was given to the Born Agains by Sagoyewatha, a Seneca chief called Red Jacket in English. Some of what he had to say should be of passing interest to the Americans bouncing around the Middle East and those responsible for sending them out there:

". . . You have now become a great people, and we have scarcely a place left to spread our blankets. You have got our country but you are not satisfied; you want to force your religion upon us.

"You say that you are sent to instruct us how to worship the Great Spirit agreeably to his mind, and, if we do not take hold of the religion which you white people teach, we shall be unhappy hereafter. You say that you are right and we are lost. How do you know this to be true? We understand that your religion is written in a book. If it was intended for us as well as for you, why has not the Great Spirit given it to us, and not only to us, but why did he not give to our forefathers the knowledge of that book, with the means of understanding it rightly? We only know what you tell us about it. How shall we know when to believe, being so often deceived by the white people?"

In the interceding two centuries Americans have lost none of their missionary chutzpah. In 2003 Condoleezza Rice, the national security advisor, had rifle and Bible out when she announced that Americans, and any others whom she could talk into it, must make a "generational commitment" to "the moral mission of our time." Which is, according to her, that ". . . America and our friends and allies must commit ourselves to a long-term transformation in . . . the Middle East . . . held back by what leading Arab intellectuals call a political and economic 'freedom deficit.' " Ms. Rice and her colleagues will determine when and how that deficit has been remedied, and anyone who objects too strenuously will be afforded an all-expense-paid sabbatical to Guantanamo Bay for the purpose of meditating and freely changing one's mind.

There is a familiar ring to this arrogance. In 1913 President Woodrow Wilson told Sir William Tyrrell, a British diplomat, "I am going to teach the South American Republics to elect good men."

Americans have a sub-abysmal record in regards to

teaching other peoples how to live properly, starting with Indians or Native Americans. The white men have killed them, but hardly tamed them, or turned them into cheap imitations of their white selves. On every peak in the great chain of mountains starting in the Aleutians and ending in Tierra del Fuego there is a group of angry, unreconciled Indians peering down into the valleys with God knows what emotions radiating out of their gaze. But at long last recompense is being made in the United States, where reparations have come in the form of casino licenses to Native American tribes who are permitted to turn the running of the gambling emporia over to crooked politicians and the Mafia, thus enabling the license holders to drink up their cut of the profits. However, in amelioration, in the years when Congress is not economizing the government pays for substance abuse counseling.

We brought the same missionary spirit to Japan when, on July 2, 1853, a flotilla of American warships showed up in Tokyo Bay to "open up" that country, which, for the previous 250 or so years, had lived in a state of *sakoku*, or national seclusion. Japan, after a not wholly satisfactory brush with Europeans and Christianity in the form of the Franciscans and Jesuits in the 16th century, had decided to shut and bar its doors to outsiders. For the next few centuries nobody got into Japan and nobody got out. That was that, or would have been if it weren't for the new, ravenously commercial republic which was growing by leaps and bounds in North America.

The Yankees wanted in and thus Commodore Matthew

Perry (1794–1858) was dispatched with a letter from President Millard Fillmore to the Japanese emperor. At this time in Japanese history the emperor had no power, a fact the American commander could not know since he had arrived in Japan with no one who could speak the language or knew the first thing about the place. (If there are elements in this episode which remind you of Iraq it is not entirely coincidental.) But cannons speak a tongue understood everywhere, so there was no misunderstanding Perry's message, which boiled down to "Let us in or we will blow your doors off their hinges." The Japanese, who had, incidentally, abandoned the use of firearms after kicking the hirsute Europeans out, acquiesced in the American ultimatum, and the two countries took the first steps down the road that would lead to the dropping of the atom bomb on Hiroshima 92 years later.

The Japanese concluded that if they were going to be forced at gun point to have congress with 19th century imperialism, they must get themselves a war fleet like the Americans'. One glance across the sea to the west and they could see how the Europeans and the Americans were tearing China apart and leaving the center of Far Eastern civilization in tatters. The Japanese mastered American technology, inspiring a popular cliché of the 1920s and 1930s: the buck-toothed, bowlegged, near-sighted Japanese tourist taking photographs of factories, military installations and other points of vital importance to a powerful industrial society. America thought of Japan as a nation of sneak thieves, spies, industrial espionage agents and business competitors. The

Japanese, in their turn, took the technology, started their own munitions industry and went to war.

A century of military occupations and what Americans call "aid" to Haiti has brought neither democracy nor prosperity but one hellacious, heart-breaking turn after another. In Cuba and the Philippines in the early years of the 20th century the United States brought to bear its civilizing influence by suppressing local self-government. Not too much blood was spilt by the meddling in Cuba, where American-style democratic institutions led to a succession of hapless governments, to people getting poorer, the foreign investors getting richer, and American organized crime getting the gambling concessions and pimping the Cuban girls to the tired businessmen from El Norte. Then Fidel Castro and the Communists arrived, and the story of this nation, derailed from whatever course it might have taken if it had been allowed self-determination, is yet to be played out.

In the Philippines, another nation whose destiny is yet to be fixed, the missionary nation-building was more sanguinary. Teddy Roosevelt, the loudest voice among the imperial visionaries who took over the country, abominated his little brown Philippine brothers, calling them "Tagal bandits . . . Chinese halfbreeds . . . savages, barbarians . . . apaches" and more. For viciousness and flouting of the rules of war, if such are to be taken seriously, the American behavior suppressing the "Philippine Insurrection" was as grizzly as anything which transpired in the Vietnam War. One soldier wrote to tell the home folks that, "last night one of our boys was found shot with his stomach cut open.

Immediately orders were received from General Wheaton to burn the town and kill every native in sight; which was done to a finish. About a thousand men and women were reported killed. I am probably growing hard-hearted for I am in my glory when I can sight my gun on some dark skin and pull the trigger."

Lessons in democracy for the people of the Philippines proceeded on principles which Palestinian Arabs will have no trouble recognizing. "If they fire a shot from a house," wrote an American trooper, "we burn the house down and every house near it, and shoot the natives so that they are pretty quiet in town now." Whether these lessons in the rule of law and representative government are responsible for it, the last fifty years of life in this nation have been constant strife. The Communist-armed insurgency after World War II has been followed by dictatorship, war-lordism and gang-sterism, and years of sporadic fighting in the southern islands between Muslim irregulars and the Philippine army and its American advisers.

During the first years of the Wilson administration (1913–1921) the gringos decided to butt into the revolutionary battle Mexicans were carrying on to rid themselves of dictatorship. After sending a succession of ad hoc diplomatic agents, ignorant of the language and the people, to meddle in the revolution, a United States naval flotilla seized the port of Vera Cruz at the cost of many Mexican lives. After Pancho Villa had raided New Mexico, killing a bunch of Americans, the United States retaliated by dispatching an army, under General John J. "Black Jack" Pershing, into the mountains and deserts of northern Mexico in a failing attempt to capture the famous revolutionary-cum-bandit. This Mexican cockup bears similarities to another American army sloshing and slashing around the Hindu Kush after Osama bin Laden.

American motives in Mexico were disinterested, as they always are. Only nations on the outside of the biosphere have selfish motives. America is the Johnnie Appleseed of democracy, spreading self-rule wherever it bombs or sends in the Marines. It is ever so, as Woodrow Wilson told the idiot bean-eaters on the south side of the Rio Grande: "We are seeking to counsel Mexico for her own good and in the interest of her own peace and not for any other purpose whatever. The government of the United States would deem itself discredited if it had any selfish or ulterior purpose in transactions where the peace, happiness and prosperity of a whole people are involved. It is acting as its friendship for Mexico, not as any self interest, dictates." Not a word about the oil, the cattle, the mineral, and the banking interests of the United States, to say nothing of the British Empire whose navy was dependent on Mexico for bunker oil to drive its new Dreadnaught-class battleships.

Wilson's missionary activities in Mexico achieved an increased hatred and resentment against the United States for its theft of California, Texas, New Mexico, Arizona, etc., and for its bullying and its interference. Revolution or no revolution, American oil and mining companies carried on as before, operating closed enclaves to which Mexican government officials were denied entrance, which paid no

taxes, built no schools, and enjoyed their imperial preroga-
tives until Mexico finally exercised its national sovereignty
and kicked the companies out, setting off talk, north of the
border, of war. Were it to have come to another American
military tourist excursion, doubtless it would have been carried out with much "public diplomacy"—the new Washington euphemism for propaganda—about how it was being
done to liberate the Mexicans from the follies of their own
self-rule.

In the colonial era, American conduct did not shock
people in other nations whose armies were doing the same
things in other places. A look at the former French, English,
Dutch, and Portugese colonies in Africa and elsewhere
makes it obvious that the American legacy is no worse but
no better. That's the point—it is not better. The Americans
stole fewer countries than some others did, and they may
not have murdered as many as did the soldiers of other
nations, who were killing not in the name of the cross and
democracy but for king, kaiser, tzar, or emperor. Call it
nation building or call it the white man's burden, the Americans were not especially bad. But they were not especially
good. When it came to raping and pillaging, they were
average, but this is not what the People of the Dome believe.

When, again under Wilson, we fought the war to end all
wars, it was to make the world safe for democracy. It was Wilson
and his principal collaborator, Herbert Hoover, who first
made generosity an instrument of foreign policy. "Food relief
is now the key to the whole European situation," Wilson
wrote. "Bolshevism is steadily advancing westward, has

overwhelmed Poland and is poisoning Germany. It cannot be stopped by force but it can be stopped by food." Wilson's thought, recast in nobler, missionary terms, was passed on to the American public by Herbert Hoover, who was in charge of the relief program: "It is America's mission, our opportunity to serve. FOOD WILL WIN THE WORLD." Wilson said that, "no man could worship God on an empty stomach," even as his secretary of state, Robert Lansing, contributed the observation that, "Full stomachs mean no Bolsheviks."

This giving away of the inventory by Uncle Sam has aggravated some Americans ever since. They cannot accept or understand that there is as much policy as there is charity in these donations. Since Wilson, foreign aid has been perfected so that it subsidizes corporate U.S. agriculture while preventing poor countries from developing profitable agriculture or feeding themselves; it shows conclusively that generosity can be a two-way street.

Regardless, an artless appeal to the missionary spirit gets a sympathetic hearing every time. Americans will quarrel over how, who, or what to rescue or save, but the idea that the nation ought to be off doing it is challenged only by a few. As the weapons of mass destruction casus belli began to wobble off course, the self-defense argument was junked and the missionary imperative was substituted. The world and the Iraqi people had to be saved from this mass murdering brute, and America, ever willing to give the lives of its young people for the freedom and safety of others, would invade Iraq, be greeted as benefactors, depose the government, and institute the reign of justice, free markets, and democratic capitalism.

You can hear the Wilsonian altruism in George Bush's speech announcing the American invasion: "We come to Iraq with respect for its citizens, for their great civilization and for the religious faiths they practice. We have no ambition in Iraq, except to remove a threat and restore control of that country to its own people." Not that we're interested in the oil in Iraq; no, America is a nation on a mission. The Reverend President spelled it out: "America has done this kind of work before. Following World War II, we lifted up the defeated nations of Japan and Germany and stood with them as they built representative governments. We committed years and resources to this cause. And that effort has been repaid many times over in three generations of friendship and peace. America today accepts the challenge of helping Iraq in the same spirit—for their sake, and our own."

Luckily, Americans are born double jointed at the shoulder which allows them to pat themselves on the back with little strain. The comforting, self-administered pats have laid to rest doubt about the future of Iraq. As the World War II song went, this will be a case of "We Did It Before And We Can Do it Again," referring to American disinterested beneficence in bringing back Japan and Germany from the ruins. Another Marshall Plan and some more innate American goodness will bring forth an Iraq which will be a model of Arab democracy at the heart of the Middle East. The New Baghdad, with running water and electricity, will cause Arabs everywhere to take one look, swoon and, as soon as smelling salts have been administered to the large nostrils of their Semitic noses (see the editorial cartoons of Arabs in the American press), to jump up, over-throw their slimy despots and establish democracies with stock market and banking laws of such crystalline trans-parency that foreign direct investment will zoom heaven-ward. Notice—not one direct mention of oil.

Nonetheless, the missionaries had second thoughts. American officials got an idea what was waiting for them the first night they bedded down in one of Saddam's palaces, though, if they'd had any sense, they would not have set foot in Iraq because they would have remembered what Dick Cheney had said years before, on February 16, 1992, after Gulf I, in a moment of clairvoyance and candor:

> If we'd gone into Baghdad . . . we'd have had to put a lot of forces in and run him (Saddam Hussein) to the ground someplace. He would not have been easy to capture. Then you've got to put a new government in his place and then you're faced with the question of what kind of government are you going to establish in Iraq? Is it going to be a Kurdish government or a Shia government or a Sunni government? How many forces are you going to have to leave there to keep it propped up, how many casualties are you going to take through the course of this operation?

Ten years later saw Cheney, Rumsfeld, and the rest of their group back in power and in Baghdad. These men had been holding one kind of high office or another for years through the Ford, Reagan, and Papa Bush administrations.

Now they were back with Boy Bush. Did they forget what they had known? In the time between Cheney's prophetic words and their ordering the American army into Iraq, had they made so much money, been flattered by so many Republican ladies, spoken at so many commencements, reviewed so many military formations that they had come to believe that creation, from man to microbe, must heed their command and fall in with their plans?

In the interim between Gulf I and Gulf II a new plan or concept was coming together. In 1992 when Cheney rejected taking over Iraq, the Soviet Union was recently gone but, like the Cheshire cat, the smile was still hanging in the air. The monomania of single, hyper-powerhood had not yet got into them and taken over their brains. They had not yet gotten used to the idea that, using America as their tool, they might be able to bully the world. When they rode Boy Bush back into government after the eight Clinton years, however, the mania had them. They were Blues Brothers on a power trip, throwing the bird to the cosmos. Their middle finger was up and they were on their way into Iraq, and once they got Iraq, they'd take over the Middle East and take the American people with them, cheering as they all went.

The project stumbled over the weapons of mass destruction, or the egregious lack thereof. There was no good reason to wage this Potemkin's war of theirs, so they found one by appealing to the missionary spirit, the abiding thought that America was set on earth to make things right.

On the other side of the dome, where mixed motives are

recognized as an ordinary part of politics, the call from the *muezzins* on the Washington minarets for a Euro-American jihad stirred few to life and arms, other than the Brits, who don't seem to realize that neither their own country nor the United States is quite so Anglo-Saxon any more. Yes, Saddam is a mass murderer and his sons were torturing sadists and his whole operation is disgustingly indefensible, but why attack him in 2003 when his murder machine had slacked off, and not fifteen years ago when he was killing thousands daily and his rape rooms were running around the clock? The tardiness of the American missionary zeal suggested other motives—which the men and women in the United Nations' lobby and the foreign offices around the would had little trouble gleaning.

15.
Why Do They Hate Us?

ELL, OF COURSE, "THEY" DON'T.

Maybe they will in the future, but even now, they don't. They have been sore tested by the U.S., but, after the heartbreaking crime of 9/11, all over the world they, with tears in their eyes, stopped Americans on the street to express their sympathies. Their governments rallied to help the United States run down everyone who abetted the murder of the doomed three thousand in the World Trade Center. An oft-quoted *Le Monde* headline said, "NOUS SOMMES TOUS AMERICAINS," and the world agreed. They know and appreciate that, with all its—shall we call them imperfections?—America is the only mass society ever to be polyglot, rich, and democratic. They also love the music. They learn American English, they don baseball caps, reverse them, and look every bit as silly as the American youths on the TV programs they watch all the time. They eat that crappy, franchise food—even the French—and delight in American's polka-dotting the planet with Disneylands. The Germans even drink Budweiser! They take part in that odious entertainment of American invention, the beauty contest. We have seeped in every-where. They couldn't get rid of us if they wanted to. We are particles in their sunbeams and fragments of their dreams— the good ones as well as the occasional nightmare. They do not hate us.

Tell that to the people of the biosphere. In truth, it is heavy lifting to tell anything to the people of the biosphere. They are so neurotically needy that they cannot listen unless it is the voice of praise, the one voice from the far side of the plex-iglass which Americans harken to. They also hear the voice of criticism. They have rabbit ears for that. It is the voice of reason which bounces off the glass.

The need for praise is almost a national vice. Other people in other countries do have things to do, like sowing seeds, harvesting potatoes, and building automobiles to export to the United States, hence sometimes the hosannas dribble off. Americans make up for these occasional praise deficits by producing spasms of self-laudification seldom seen since Louis XIV. Louis, the Sun King, specialized in flashing his golden glory to keep the common folk abashed and abased; dictators indulge in gorgeous militaristic festi-vals, balancing bad economies with hot air and rhetoric instead of ample food and a healthy diet. Americans have their non-stop talk-a-thon about being the greatest country in the world, the richest, the freest, the most religious, wisest, the bravest, land of opportunity, etc., which embarrasses others and has finally given America a case of macrocephaly, or fat-headedness. The people outside the dome know that America has had marvelous moments and every so often has come near to being the country it claims to be, but they also know, which Americans don't, that this is one of the nation's down periods and that makes the bragging all the more divisive. They don't hate us, but even as they admire America for so much they see us for what we are.

Whenever Americans are afflicted with a twinge of doubt or sense the dislike of others, real or supposed, they take a public opinion survey which confirms that "they" hate us. This headline in the *New York Times* is illustrative: "U.S. Asks Muslims Why It Is Unloved. Indonesians Reply." The lead in the story reads, "A group of Indonesian Muslims, handpicked by the United States Embassy here for their moderate views, this week told an expert panel from Washington in unvarnished terms why America is unloved in the Islamic world." Lesson number one on how to live in your own hermetically sealed globe.

If anybody ever believed in *vox populi vox dei* it is the Americans. The tanks and the Humvees had no sooner parked in central city, Baghdad, than American persons or American-sponsored persons, clipboards in hand, were to be seen making their way through the reeds on the sides of the Tigris River looking for people to question. Do you feel more liberated now than last year? On a scale of one to ten locate your feelings about the United States, one being unalloyed hatred and ten unadulterated love. Does your family own a weapon of mass destruction? If yes, did you build it yourself?

Polling and other forms of politically social inquiry will net the answers the questioners are hoping for. Polling, in the hands of but a few, is an elaborate way of confirming pre-conceptions, of thinking one has swung open the glass door of the biosphere when actually one is still inside, breathing re-circulated air. In spite of the whoop-de-do communications theories and ever-advancing survey techniques, the constant complaint of people on the other side of the windows is that Americans simply won't listen. They won't listen to being told they won't listen and, when they are told, it increases their neediness for praise and their belief that they are hated. Such talk fans the feeling of being disliked or not liked enough. If the IV praise drip is stopped, the persecution complex kicks in.

A routine has been perfected in which Americans go to international conferences, attack what's going on, announce they will not abide by the conferences decisions, place themselves above, beyond, and outside rules and obligations agreed to by many other nations and then go into angry paranoia mode when people from the beyond answer them with criticism and irritation. Everybody, except the British, are after them. They see bogeymen crawling in the windows and pouring through keyholes of the doors. The Americans and the Israelis, another bunch which holds little brief for multi-national cooperation, are the only winners in the world with a persecution complex. Behold America, and its little Middle Eastern twin, bristling with nuclear devices, advanced weapon systems, absolute air and naval domination, tanks the size of barns zipping across the countryside, and yet the Americans cower in the corner, positive that super forces—which must be from outer space because there are none so strong as they on earth—are mobilizing to smash them. The people outside the dome understand that the United States is so powerful that it is invulnerable, absolutely undefeatable. Inside the dome Americans are convinced that their country could be destroyed by al Qaeda and the other terrorists, but hysterical America is unmindful that the 9/11 massacre, appalling and infinitely sad as it is, was less than a shaving nick out of the gross domestic product. In terms of people it was awful; in terms of lost wealth and power, it was a mosquito bite.

16

Unconditional Surrender

THERE WAS NOT ONLY a stillness at Appomattox, there was also unconditional surrender. The Southern side had to give up completely. No ands, ifs, or buts. No treating with or talking to any Confederate government. The surrender would be unconditional, the extirpation of any trace of what brought the South into rebellion.

Given the circumstances, unconditional surrender made sense, and it has lurked around times of conflict ever since. Something close to it was achieved in the Spanish-American War with the Spaniards happy to sign any piece of paper and get out with a payment of Yankee money for the Philippines, as if they had the right to sell somebody's country and the United States had the right to buy it. World War I ended with less than a formal unconditional surrender, but with the German and Austrian governments dissolved and disappeared, as if they had been abolished by a conqueror.

In World War II unconditional surrender was openly proclaimed as the only basis on which the United States would cease hostilities. As a battle cry, unconditional surrender has a certain bracing ring to it, but as statecraft it leaves much to be desired. It made it difficult for German anti-Nazis or non-Nazis to get rid of Hitler and sue for some kind of negotiated peace, but that point of view cut no ice in Washington, where the guilt of the German people was a popular point of view. Within eighteen months of the unconditional surrender, and in view of the Communist threat, the German people were found to be not entirely guilty after all.

Nevertheless, unconditional surrender more or less worked out.

In Korea it did not. The Korean War was begun after the North Koreans, then a new-born Communist state no more than five years old, for no good reason invaded South Korea, a non-communist, non-democratic state of similar age. America, working through the United Nations, came to the southerners defense and drove the invaders out of South Korea. At that point the Americans, having restored the *status quo ante*, might have left, but the decision was taken to punish North Korea by invading it with an eye to abolishing it entirely and reuniting the two Korean halves. Unconditional surrender was in the air, but as the American forces came close to realizing their goal, they were attacked by the Chinese Communists, whose army forced the Americans back to the border which separates the two Koreas to this day.

The United States also went into Vietnam looking for

unconditional surrender, even after seeing the French colonial forces there defeated. But the froggies can't fight and they don't like Americans and we don't like them, so there was nothing to be learned from that quarter. During the opening of the American part of the Indochina War, the Americans acted as though to say, "The big boys are on the scene now, and no more crap will be taken from Commie gooks." Terms were laid out and they were simple: The Communists were to amscray out of South Vietnam and there was nothing more to talk about. Years of fighting bent the Americans around to wanting to negotiate, which they finally did, concluding an agreement with the Communists that was something of a sell-out of the South.

The idea of unconditional surrender has a deleterious effect on American strategy. It assumes that a total military victory will be gained and the dispute settled without give-and-take politics. It means no negotiation. It means that you do what I say because you have been annihilated, you are powerless and I have my foot on your neck. This was the American reaction to the Japanese sneak attack on Pearl Harbor and it is the American reaction to the al Qaeda attack on the World Trade Center. Thus, as the War on Terrorism, which had been bubbling along before, was kicked up into the be-all-and-end-all of life at the White House, the mad dogs of terror would be hunted down one by one and killed—which sounds good assuming a finite number of mad dogs and no new mad dogs enlisting in the terror.

The kill-every-last-one-of-'em approach was first tried out in Afghanistan. Not only was the al Qaeda nest to be

bunker bombed but the Taliban, the de facto government of
Afghanistan which existed in no small measure because of
prior American support, was to be x-ed out of history. At no
juncture in the Afghan assault was any thought given to
finding out if the Taliban was up for negotiation. Would
they, for instance, turn over Osama bin Laden and his pals
to the United States in return for a cessation of hostilities?
No such thought was possible because, on top of the anger
caused by 9/11, missionary righteousness intervened. The
Taliban governed Afghanistan by the strictest, and, from a
western point of view, most ghastly code of law. There were
women in peonage, maimings for punishment, beatings on
the street administered to music lovers, and more. By our
standards the Taliban had joined the not-too-select company of rulers who have made their countries hell on earth.
But none of their policies had any particular connection
with 9/11 save that they had al Qaeda guests, but guests can
be disinvited. Instead the Taliban were to be destroyed.

When Cato, the Elder, ended every speech on every subject in the Roman senate with the words "*Delenda carthago
est*," or "Carthage must be destroyed," he meant the whole
place, the whole people, and when that was done by the
Roman general Scipio, they poured salt over the area so
nothing would grow there. That is unconditional surrender,
but what happened in Afghanistan was unconditional surrender without the destruction of the enemy. It was Grant at
Appomattox without Lee. There was no peace and nobody
to negotiate with. It was a mess.

Unconditional surrender was tried again in Iraq. Again

nobody from the other side turned up to sign the papers. Short of doing what Cato and Scipio did—that is, destroying the country and driving the people out— America bought itself anarchy and confusion while terrorism and the war against the same did or did not go on as before. No can say because a war against terrorism is a war against nameless people who may or may not exist at any given moment. If the battlefield communiques from the government in an ordinary war are read with incredulity, dispatches from an invisible war are absolutely not to be trusted. A war against named people or named organizations is perhaps a winnable war, but a war against terrorism is like a war against a state of mind. How would you know if and when you may have won it? When there are no bombings? Years elapsed between the first and second attacks on the World Trade Center, during which there were no bombings in the United States. The war against terrorism thus defined means you cannot know when you have won, or if you have won. The absence of violence reveals nothing except there was no bombing today. A generation or more would have to pass before people would begin to say, "Gee, I guess we won." Ten minutes later a bomb might go off in a movie theater.

September 11 justifies the unreasoning anger which makes unconditional surrender reasonable. Only hydrophobic beasts would murder all those people, so they must be hunted down to the last man, except the men who did the deed are dead themselves and the only beasts left are the beasts and the uberbeasts who put the homi-suicidal idea in the dead men's heads. But are those animals driven only by hate and hell? Is that their full story? Do they have no war aims? No reason to fight besides hating Americans and Israelis just because they do? Are they practitioners of a blood cult or do they use terror for something other than a diabolic catharsis peculiar to Muslims? Given the premise of the unconditional surrender policy, which makes the war against terrorism a rabid animal hunt, no other end can come about except killing all of them, whoever and how many of them there may be.

Outside the dome the roots of the war, in which one side kills non-combatants because it is too weak to kill its enemy's soldiers, are seen as something more complicated than infection of the meninges. Elsewhere people can see that there is a political foundation to the conflict, and that suggests the possibility of political solutions achieved by negotiation. Within the dome, it's still unconditional surrender or war, if not everlasting, then lasting for a long, long time.

17.
Self Portrait

NSIDE THE TERRARIUM THERE is a constant drip of reassurance as the people are praised for their gallantry and told that they are a besieged breed battling for human rights. Mostly they battle the traffic on the way home from the office, but the air is heavy with reports of continuous, ongoing strife. It's all struggles and war: against cancer, teen drinking, teen pregnancy, drugs, illiteracy, terrorism, child abuse, drunk driving, diabetes, rape of the environment, pornography, starvation in less developed countries, ignorance, poverty, intolerance, heart disease, AIDS.

When they look into their mirrors, do Americans see tough, brave faces, heads wound round with bloody bandages? Do they hear, from the speakers blaring from every elevator and in every shopping mall, the martial beat of the drum, the toot of a flute, and "Yankee Doodle Dandy"?

Every year thousands dress up in 18th- and 19th-century military uniforms to reenact battles of the Revolutionary and Civil Wars in which the good and the brave win and suffer no casualties. They do not reenact the big battles of the 20th century, those of the Somme or of Kursk, where hundreds of thousands perished. Innocent of knowledge of the terrible slaughters of more recent history, America's heroes don camouflage suits and spend weekends bouncing about the countryside fighting paint-ball battles.

The men who fought at Iwo Jima and Normandy are entering their eighties; the men who fought in the Mekong Delta are into their fifties. The people younger than these veterans, now more than half the population, have no memories and no experience of those violent rampages. Their wars are Rambo and the other heart-stopping celluloid foolishness where we are young and brave forever.

They enroll in survivalist programs, join camouflage jump suit cults, play x-games. Those who don't join in the actual outdoor activities watch on television, not infrequently inside a thirty-foot, air-conditioned, motorized trailer with an HDTV satellite dish, parked on a camping site in a manicured wilderness with a view. They are "toughing it," convinced, as are most Americans, that they are undergoing the adversity which builds character and leadership. Fed by the television ads, Americans wobble between a past which never was and a present which never will be. It is a fantasy life nobody else shares.

Work has its own place in the national theology. Working till you drop in the traces wins you a patch of ground among

the honored dead. The work ethic beats out the peace ethic
or the love ethic. The blue collar man is the best kind of
man. Can you hear the factory whistle blowing? Can you see
him with his lunch pail and square-toed, high top shoes?
The fixation on work has Americans believing that the
people on the other side of the terrarium walls are drones.
The long vacations taken by the French and the Germans
are a species of immorality, the low stress social life of the
Nordics is decadent and economically degenerate. Other
people don't put in enough time on the job, which makes
America the straining Atlas of the Rockefeller Center statue,
holding up the world.

The Atlas of Greek mythology was stuck keeping the
world up over his head as a punishment for having taken the
wrong side in the battle with the Titans. This Atlas believes
that he is being punished for having taken the right side and
gotten nothing for it but grief, ingratitude and the burden of
running the world. Europe's ingratitude is a stock theme in
politicians' speeches and editorials. It is like sour cud,
brought up repeatedly to show how unappreciated America
is for all it has done for others, and how little others have
done for it. The people in the dome insistently repeat that
twice, three times if you count keeping out communism,
America has saved Europe, but no one is grateful. No one
gives a helping hand to Atlas when he tears a meniscus or
rips a tendon while protecting the peoples of the earth.
Since others won't recognize the debt, a resentful America
memorializes itself in an outpouring of books and movies
and patriotic half-time shows in the football stadiums where

sports fans are comforted by the reminder that they live in a land of selfless heroism.

The past we know is the past we need for the present we have; it shows us an idealistic, altruistic, heroic America ready to lay down the lives of its children for others, though the beneficiaries may not appreciate the sacrifices made for them. For such purposes World War II is of precious memory for it was—we remind you—the good war, the right war, the unambiguous war, the Manichean war of us versus pure evil. It may have been so, but many an American then was not too keen to fight it. That past, too, has been prettied-up for current requirements.

Franklin Roosevelt won reelection in 1940 by promising that Americans wouldn't fight the good war. When Hitler invaded Poland in 1939, America did not rush to arms as the British and French did. More than two years went by before the United States went to war. Had Pearl Harbor not been bombed and had Hitler not declared war on the United States at the same time, America might have stayed neutral and let the Nazis win.

Now World War II is big again. *Saving Private Ryan* and a slew of propaganda efforts create a semi-fictional past which is used as a basis for a semi-tragic present. The greatest generation did what history asked of it, but it was not all for one and one for all. As valiantly as the soldiers fought, war-time America was also black-market America. Senator Harry Truman made the reputation which won him the vice presidential nomination in 1944 by investigating crooked war contractors.

Earlier, in 1917, many believed that the United States wasn't going to war to save Europe but to save the Morgan banking interests. Morgan had made loans to Great Britain which would default if the other side won. When President Wilson asked Congress for a declaration of war against imperial Germany, his words were not taken as a call for a self-sacrificing crusade by all the senators. Nebraska's Republican George Norris told the nation, "Belligerency would benefit only the class of people who will be made prosperous should we become entangled in the present war, who have already made millions of dollars, and who will make hundreds of millions more if we get into the war . . . We are going into war upon the command of gold . . . I feel that we are about to put the dollar sign on the American flag." His fellow senators shouted, "Treason!", but Norris was one of the rare ones, willing to say what many others thought—that the war was not about saving Europe but about saving some people's money. Although the modern Senate had no George Norris to say it, there were those who thought the Iraqi invasion was war on the command of oil. There's an old bromide: when they say it isn't the money, it's the money. When they say it isn't the oil, is it the oil? Stories of corruption and fixed deals usually start circulating after a war has been going on for a while, but this time people were sniffing out an oily smell on Dick Cheney and certain people in the Pentagon before the first American tank rumbled across the Iraqi border.

Most decades have their crooked big-shot politicians. They swarmed the Harry Truman administration; Richard

Nixon's vice president, Spiro Agnew, collected bribe money in his White House office; Bill Clinton sold pardons. But you have to go back to the 19th century, to Schuyler Colfax (1823–1885), for a vice president with the same unrepentant, truculent, stiff-necked money hunger Dick Cheney exhibits. Taking Credit Mobilier railroad corporate stock gained Colfax a degree of immortality as the archetypal betrayer of the public trust. Doing much the same is Cheney's best shot for a place of comparable importance on the History Channel.

18.
Terrorism

T HE WORD DATES FROM the 18th century and was first applied to the actions of the government of the French Revolution. It derives from *La Terreur*, the name given to the time between May 31, 1793, when the sanguinary Maximilien de Robespierre assumed dictatorial power over the Revolution, and July 27, 1794 when he went to the same death he had prepared for so many others. Since then, the word has been applied to murders and killings and horrific acts of violence of all kinds by all kinds of people from all kinds of organizations with all kinds of motives. Like pornography and urban sprawl, nobody can define terrorism but everybody recognizes it when they see it—or so they say.

The simple act of slitting the throat, even of a suckling mother, is not necessarily terrorism. It's terrible, but that's different. Terrorism is not defined by the guilt—or lack thereof—of its victims. If it were, virtually every government in the world would be seen as using terrorism on a daily basis.

The act may be murder but once it is called terrorism, it has been placed in a political, not a criminal, category. People who support the goals of a terrorist campaign call the killing guerilla warfare. Killing thus labeled is legit. The taxonomical game is played with countries. If Syria, for instance, is being naughty in the eyes of the speaker, Syria is a "rogue nation." If Syria is doing the exact same naughtiness but the speaker approves of it, Syria is a "valued member of the international community."

Because the only useful definitions of terrorism are political, the label is not a permanent one. Once a terrorist, war lord, or bandit, not always a terrorist, war lord, or bandit. The Mau Mau terrorists became the government of Kenya. The Irish terrorists in Belfast are on their way to taking over as the legitimate government. Nelson Mandela and Gandhi were once regarded as terrorists by the British and the South African governments. Similar examples are legion. The Maquis, the French underground resistence against the Germans in World War II, were guerilla fighters or terrorists, depending on which side you were on. In North America, a number of Indian tribes or nations were so regarded by the United States. Some terrorists never do get their labels switched and die the death of the outsider. But you never know. The terrorist you condemn today may be the respected personage you are sitting next to at a testimonial dinner tomorrow. Winning gets you a tuxedo and a seat at the table every time.

Terrorists and guerilla fighters have been romanticized in times past. The 19th-century French terrorist caught some of that frequently misguided admiration with the remark, *"Qu'importe les victimes, si le geste est beau."* Phrases like "the propaganda of the deed" have been flung around by those who invested an almost metaphysical value in their killings, and time has given the anarchist bomb throwers of a hundred years ago a certain, often specious, appeal, but a glance around the modern world will tell anybody with a decent pair of eyes that most terrorist/guerillas are swine. Most are unlike Osama bin Laden, who—regardless of the enormity of the acts attributed to him or the Palestinian terrorists, who have wreaked a horrific toll on the young, the old and the helpless—fight for a cause. Most terrorists fight for loot, for ugly power, for rape, torture and crimes which used to be unspeakable but now can be read about in the daily press outside of the dome. Inside the dome, if it's unpleasant, we don't want to hear about it.

No single act of death-dealing terrorism comparable to 9/11 comes readily to mind, but terrorism of one kind or another is an old song and, although Americans think of it as a recent, noxious import, it has been around a long time. In the United States terrorism began in the 1870s in the coal fields of Pennsylvania and shook the country to its foundations in 1886, when a person or persons unknown tossed a bomb into a group of police in Chicago's Haymarket Square, killing seven of them. For the next three decades bombings and assassination attempts punctuated public life in America. When Franklin Roosevelt was

Undersecretary of the Navy during World War I, a terrorist tried to plant a bomb under the house of the attorney general, A. Mitchell Palmer, who lived across the street from Roosevelt. As happens often today, the bomber goofed while in the act and blew himself up, sending his body parts flying every which way and leaving a severed thumb on FDR's lawn.

Although when they hear the word, Americans think of Arabs, Arabs of the modern era are late-comers to terrorism. It was practiced in the latter half of the 19th and throughout the 20th century across Northern and Southern Europe, the Balkans, South America, and even by Israelis against the English and against the Arabs in the years before their nation had been established.

There is an apothegm that terrorism never pays off, but it is not so. It did not prevent the Zionists in old Palestine from gaining victory and establishing the State of Israel, the IRA did all right with it in Northern Ireland, and other instances of terrorism of one sort or another which worked out just fine for the terrorists can be found without much digging.

The underground forces at war with Israel have used terrorism for years, and after each incident they are roundly condemned and invited to condemn themselves, which Yasir Arafat sometimes does and sometimes doesn't. Terrorists are told on American television talks shows that they are "only hurting their own cause" by resorting to acts of terror. The same thing was said when Dr. Martin Luther King, Jr., kicked up trouble. The television personalities would say that "He is only setting his cause back" by boycotting or sitting down in the street. The members of a cause may or may not be the best judges of the efficacy of their tactics, but they are the only judges whom supporters of the cause dare trust.

Have the Palestinians hurt their cause by terror? Before you can answer that question, there is a prior one which needs addressing: Where would the Palestinians be if they had eschewed terror? Would they have been allowed to keep their olive orchards and would they have been given a nice comfy little state with schools and hospitals and its own government?

Generally, terrorism is used by the relatively powerless against the relatively powerful. The other way around is not terrorism. Powerful countries do things which, if done by a group hiding out in the jungles of Peru, would be called terrorism. France, England, the old Soviet Union, through their various secret services, have engaged in acts which, if done by others, would be denounced as terrorism. The Israeli government is famous for it (though not under the dome), and, of course, the CIA is credited with a list of vile acts in the defense of liberty.

Blowing up a café in Tel Aviv and killing children eating ice cream with their parents who are drinking café latte is terrorism. Pot-shooting a Palestinian boy walking in an olive grove is not; that is defending Israel's right to exist. Preventing ten thousand Iraqi children from getting proper nutrition is not; that is fighting for freedom.

Terrorism is against the rules and those who use it are not fighting fair. The rules are made by status quo governments at big meetings in Switzerland. By definition to fight fair you have to be fighting for a country, meaning a sovereign entity with at least enough clout to issue postage stamps. Therefore, according to dome reckoning, violence perpetrated by an Arab is, a priori, terrorism. No distinctions are allowed, but if they were, some distinctions would intrigue those with a mischievous turn of mind.

In October 1983, 241 United States Marines were killed in Lebanon in what is always called a terrorist attack when the incident is brought up. The Marines were in Lebanon in support of an Israeli invasion of the hapless country, which resulted in the deaths of thousands of Lebanese and Palestinian refugees as well as the destruction of much of Beirut by Israeli artillery bombardment. The Israelis had invaded Lebanon with Ariel Sharon metaphorically in the lead tank, in one of their attempts to extirpate Yasir Arafat and the PLO rather than negotiate with them. Although the Americans, as per usual, had styled themselves as honest brokers/peace keepers/neutrals, the local residents looked on them as invaders and were attacking any and everything that was an American governmental presence. The Marines were in a war zone and they were killed by a suicide bomber. By definition it was an act of terrorism; by common sense it would have been defined as an act of war successfully carried out because of the incompetence of the Marine officers in command, who had all their men sleeping in one dormitory in the middle of a war. In retaliation, President Ronald Reagan dusted off an old World War II battleship and sent it to shell Lebanese and Syrian military positions as American jets dropped their bombs on them.

In October 2000 the Marine incident was repeated on water when an American man of war, the U.S.S. *Cole*, refueling off the coast of Yemen, was attacked by two suicide bombers in a tiny boat and grievously damaged. Seventeen sailors were killed. Again, the finger pointed at terrorism, although, once more, it was clear that the ship was in a war zone and thus might have taken steps to see that little dynamite-laden skiffs did not come alongside and blow them to kingdom come. Throughout the 90s, there were suicide attacks on American embassies and other installations in Nairobi, Kenya, Dar al-Salaam, Tanzania, and Saudi Arabia, causing a shockingly high number of deaths. Each came as much as a surprise as the last to an American government which has had, even after the mess in Iraq, an inability to recognize that it had some years before made itself a combatant, a party at war, an invader. It was not as it pictured itself, a bizarre armed charity or the world's first eleemosynary war machine.

On the other side of the dome, it was obvious to Europeans and Africans and Arabs everywhere that the United States had, by some time in the 1980s, made itself a de facto belligerent in the perpetual under-and-over ground wars in Israel/Palestine and the Gulf regions. By defining strikes against itself as acts of terror directed against an innocent, neutral, peaceful third party, the people inside the dome are surprised every time they are blindsided by their adversaries. Then comes the indignant clucks and the truculent screeches as bombs and missiles are fired off in all directions, hitting God knows whom. The Americans have been at war for years without acknowledging it. After 9/11 it was acknowledged. Bush declared war against terrorism, which is about as precise and useful as declaring war against the Atlantic Ocean.

In this era the suicide bomber, the warrior who goes into his or her battle one hundred per cent sure that they will die, is the face of terrorism. Undeterred by any calculation of risk, this fighter unnerves potential targets who know that these killers will contemplate what others wouldn't think of attempting. The news of so many suicide fighters spooked Americans. It confirmed the suspicion that Muslims were irrational fanatics, a foul breath expelled from the belly of the Middle Ages into modern times. The civilized way of war is to go into battle believing you will survive it, though a visit to a military cemetery would provide evidence that there is not too much difference between the two internal warrior modalities. American miliary history is chock-a-block with tales of suicidal heroism, such as the marine pilot at the Battle of Midway in 1942 who dove his plane on to a Japanese warship.

As suicide bombing came to the fore, it was first explained as stupid Arab youths beguiled by their stupid religion's stupid promise of sex with virgin girls in return for throwing their lives away. Next, the psychology of suicide bombing was explained by the prevalence of poverty and lack of indoor plumbing, but as more suicide bombers did their bloody work and were revealed to be persons from a variety of stations in life, some poor, some professionals, men and women, Bush's explanations for why America was being attacked got cloudier and more inane. Finally he was reduced to saying that they "hate freedom."

Since the government could not come up with a believable motive, it has concentrated on terrorist acts, both those already committed and the horrible things terrorists may do in the future. Scaring the hell out of everybody is a tactic used not only by Bush's people but one also employed by Clinton's. One of the more risible stories of the Clinton period was the New York *Times* report that "Defense Secretary William Cohen appeared on television brandishing a bag of sugar in an effort to describe how small a dose of biological and chemical weapons it would take to threaten Americans . . ."

American officials, even after 9/11 and the kindness of others, complained that other governments do not take the threat of terrorism seriously. Had the foreigners gone through a World Trade Center catastrophe, they would have the same urgency about terrorism that Americans do. Once more, two different realities are at play. In many parts of Europe Muslims and Arabs are not the puzzling exotics they are in the United States. People know something about them and about what they think. Thus, not surprisingly, outside the dome the proposition that a large number of Arabic persons woke up one morning chanting, "We hate freedom. Kill Americans," was improbable. That so many would be infected with such a virulent case of homicidal psycho pathology they would kill themselves acting it out had few takers.

Outside the terrarium, terrorism is regarded as an extension of politics, not psychiatry. The war of terrorism, waged primarily against the United States and Israel, is viewed as political regardless of how mistaken, wrong-headed, or shocking the reasons and manner of waging it may be. Having had to contend with politically inspired terrorism, usually motivated by nationalist ambitions and religious differences, they know that this kind of struggle can go on for decades and is seldom suppressed by military means alone. What they look for from the United States and do not see is a political component in the war against the shadowy terrorists. No attempt is made to contact the other side, there is no negotiating position because there are no negotiations. There is not even the publication of a political program which might entice the terrorists into considering taking up a different occupation. The rest of the world, European, Muslim, whoever, watches the United States commit acts which make it the number one recruiter for a new generation of terrorists. Skeptical that the mailed fist will eradicate the danger, others continue to help the United States track down these dangerous men and women but with the fear that, if force alone is the American answer, for each terrorist who is caught before he does his deed, two more are aborning.

19.
Conspiracy

A CONSPIRACY IS TWO OR more people joined together to do something you disapprove of.

As such, conspiracies abound. Some conspiracies do not exist. The alleged conspiracy which has it that George Bush is responsible for 9/11 is not true, though propounded around the globe. Judging from his track record as a failed businessman and bumbling public official, if President Bush had conspired to bring off 9/11, the World Trade Center would still be standing.

The Council on Foreign Relations is suspected of conspiring to bring about world government. If true, it goes to prove you don't have to worry about most conspiracies.

Are there more conspiracies than there used to be? Probably, because there are more people than there used to be.

Do conspiracies have to be secret? We have no knowledge of secret conspiracies because they are secret, but very few people can a keep a secret. On the day of his murder, apparently the only person in Rome who was not hip to the plan was Julius Caesar.

What can people do to prevent or protect themselves against conspiracies? Watch the pea, not the shells.

20.

Les Arabes

NO LESS THAN 22 separate nations are classified as Arab. There are millions of Arabs in France, which may help explain why the non-Arab French have hung back on some of the better Middle East bombing runs. Arabs live in Great Britain. Arabs are numerous; they are coming up on two hundred million in total numbers. They are all over, except inside the terrarium where they don't exist and nobody's ever heard of them.

When an American looks at the space being occupied by an Arab, he doesn't see anything. They are non-people with a non-claim to nothing. The non-est of the non-people are the so-called Palestinians, who do not exist at all. Israeli Prime Minister Golda Meir once summed up the absence of anything like a Palestinian people when she said, "It is not as though there were a Palestinian people in Palestine considering itself as a Palestinian people." Since America more or less takes its cue as to what to think, believe, and do in the Middle East from Israel, Palestinianism is not going to make much headway in the USA, nor has it. As an Arab subset, they are invisible interlopers.

In peace and war, even before Charlemagne's grandfather, Charles Martel, defeated Abd-er-Rahman at the Battle of Tours in 732 AD, Europeans have included Arabs in their earthly cosmology. Unlike the people of the dome, they talk to Arabs, sometimes even in Arabic, they trade with them and, occasionally, they may find an Arab they like. Arabs exist for them. They don't for Americans, who define them as nomadic nobodies with no homeland. Outside the dome, preponderant opinion extends basic rights to them; within the dome, Americans can be embarrassed into saying that Arabs have rights, but they don't mean it. In America, if you have an Arab friend, keep track of him. He can vanish in a minute and it may be years later that you learn the government has outfitted him in a striking orange jump suit and provided him with food and lodging on a razor-wired tropical isle.

Oil will induce Americans to focus on Arabs, but this is not good news for Arabs. Americans resent that Arabs, camel persons of no fixed abode, get to have all that oil and that America is increasingly dependent on it. What has the Arab done to deserve billions and billions of barrels of sweet crude? At one time America produced all the oil it needed and exported a surplus. Warnings, repeatedly made, that oil profligacy would ultimately cause the United States to look abroad for supplies, went unheeded. The motto was "Drain

America Dry," and that's what happened. Nothing was done
to use the domestic oil supply more prudently, and so the
day came when America had to start importing crude. Now
it imports most of what it uses.

It is possible that America has significant oil and gas
reserves it has not availed itself of. These lie in Alaska, off
the coast of California and elsewhere in some of the lower-
48, government-owned wilderness areas. Tapping these
deposits might injure and even destroy various plants and
animals, to say nothing about what exploitation might do to
the beauty of the sites. The right thing to do is buy oil from
Saudi Arabia and to hell with their ecology. To hell with
their plants and their animals, if those retromingent camel
jockeys have any plants or animals. Should Arab oil lands be
turned into oily muck or a gooey wasteland, it is of small
consequence because nobody lives there unless you count
Arabs, and we don't count Arabs.

If challenged on this thesis, its proponents will say that oil
is "the common heritage of mankind." All oil? Well, no, not
California oil or Texas oil or Oklahoma oil, no, not that oil.
But Arab oil, that oil should be pumped and managed with
an eye to price levels which make money for oil companies
and are satisfactory to industrial users and commuters in
California and New York. No free market and no profit max-
imization for Arab oil. The prices and amount pumped
should be decided by some kind of "command economy"
calculation of the kind once used by the Soviet Union, thus
ensuring the people of the dome will have cheap oil, because
energy conservation is not an option.

Since Saudi Arabia has the most oil, it gets the most resentment. The carping and criticism aimed at them is non-stop. They got rich taking our money; they are parasites; they use the money we pay them for oil to subsidize terrorists; they use the money we pay them for oil to buy Mercedes Benz automobiles and live in vulgar and excessive luxury, unlike the Texas oil tycoons of the past who gave the world lessons in taste and self-restraint. Oil Arabs do not save their money; oil Arabs do not know how to handle money; they waste money; they are not really entitled to the money because they did not earn it.

Under the rubrics of a free-market capitalism, when a customer is dissatisfied with a seller, he takes his business elsewhere. However, there is a porismatically-derived theorem from this statement called the Arab Exception. It says that if you think the Arabs are charging too much for their oil or they are not pumping fast enough, take their goddamn oil. Boycotts or others forms of refusal to sell oil by Arabs are not allowed by the Arab Exception.

Since the ascension of Bush II and his jolly confederates, talk of war against Saudi Arabia has been daily chatter. If an invasion of Saudi Arabia is decided on, the reasons will be: 1) To prevent Saudi use of their weapons of mass destruction; 2) To ensure that women have the right to drive in Ryiadh; 3) To make the schools coeducational; 4) To make sure Saudi girls can compete in the Miss Universe Contest; 5) To encourage Saudis of both genders to find another religion.

What Americans think about Arabs is reflected in

American motion pictures, as seen in such offerings as
Road to Morocco (1942), *Ilsa: Harem Keeper of the Oil
Sheiks* (1976), and the unspeakable *Ishtar* (1987). Jack G.
Shaheen has undertaken the thankless job of going
through hundreds, if not thousands, of films in which
Arabs appear, no matter how briefly, to get an overview of
how Arabs have been depicted at the box office for the
last century. His conclusion is that the Arab "has always
been the cultural 'other.' Seen through Hollywood's dis-
torted lens Arabs look different and threatening . . . From
1896 until today, film makers have collectively indicted all
Arabs as Public Enemy Number One—brutal, heartless,
uncivilized religious fanatics and money-mad cultural
'others' bent on terrorizing civilized Westerners, especially
Christians and Jews."

Wherever Arabs are, they are always where they ought not
to be. If they are not pitching their tents over other people's
oil, then they are gumming up the holy sites of other people's
religions. This is the united opinion of Jewish and Christian
divines, who resent the non-people for having filtered into
Jerusalem and adjacent precincts at one time or another and
who now claim that some of these places are *their* holy sites,
too. As if Arabs could have sacred sites.

It is only in modern times that Jews, the crazy ones that
is, now armed with the State of Israel's nuclear bombs and
other weapons of mass destruction, have killed Arabs over
religious sites, especially the Temple Mount. Apparently,
in one of the holy books it is written that, "My God is a
real estate God and whosoever dareth to foreclose on His

Property shall shortly feel the tip of a missile up his ying-yang." If inspirational texts do not provide justification for kicking the Arab shepherds off their hills, Moses had better climb back up that mountain for further instructions. From outside the dome this twisted take on reality looks like insanity, but, from inside, the right thing to do is to snatch Arab acreage, arrange for hundreds of thousands of squatters to plump down on it, and drive the children of Satan with their camels, their sheep, and their goats out into the waterless desert to meet whatever future may be waiting for them.

Christians have been killing Arabs for occupying their holy places for a long, long time. From the 11th through the 14th centuries the Christian Church sent army after army into the Holy Land to commit Saracen souls to eternal damnation and to claim or re-claim, as they would have had it, the Holy Land. The Crusades were a mainstream religious activity in which popes, emperors, kings, and other top drawer elements of medieval society were the driving powers behind the continuous assaults on the Arabs. Viewed from the 21st century, the Crusades may now be seen as aggression akin to the invasion of Iraq, but nine hundred years ago the respectable people, the sane ones, were behind it much as many under the dome are behind invading a lengthening list of Arab nations today.

In America the Christian denominations which have been called mainstream in the past are increasingly no-stream. They are drying up and shriveling here, as they are in Europe. With the waning influence of the denominations that conduct their services in Gothic edifices, power and public respectability have passed to the wingnut or foozball branches of American Christianity, where it is held that the Second Coming of Jesus Christ demands driving Arabs out of the general area of Palestine; a goal which, regardless of its theological merits, ultimately led to the invasion of Iraq. It is believed by the religious crazies, among whose number apparently is the President of the United States, that the presence of Arabs and their al Aqsa Mosque on the Temple Mount or Noble Sanctuary in the old quarter of Jerusalem is holding up the beginning of Armageddon, the arrival of the anti-Christ for a seven-year period called the "rapture," which ends when Christ, the genuine article, returns to fight for Israel. If this stuff reads like the plot of an action figure cartoon, thousands are dying because of it.

Europe, after centuries of struggle to disentangle throne from altar, has become secular, moderate, tolerant, and skeptical of the recurrent storms of superstitious belief which America suffers from. In no area of life is the reality inside the biosphere and outside it more divergent. Outside, people continue to admire past American accomplishments in material achievement and political imagination, even as they worry that much is in jeopardy of being canceled out by a government and society increasingly dominated by Judeo-Christian schemes of violence and death.

If a way could only be found to deal with the Arab problem. Certain laboratories are working to perfect a process for converting Arabs into crude oil. Scientists are hopeful that they will soon have a pilot plant making oil at a ten to one ratio, that is ten Arabs to produce a barrel of crude. Since Arabs have a high birth rate, this technology will make crude oil a renewable energy resource. Beyond the ecological and economical benefits, SUV drivers will feel more than a surge of acceleration when they put the pedal to the metal and reflect that Ali and Ibrahim and Osama and the rest of al Qaeda are flying out of their tail pipes.

21.
Mooslims

ILL A HOLIDAY CARD of the future depict ye olde New England snow scene of yore with the horse drawn sledge carrying the Christmas tree past a classic steepled church and a mosque with minaret? The Three Wise Men in those creches which the American Civil Liberties Union is forever getting booted off the lawn in front of city hall are dressed like Arabs, and there may be a camel or two, but no Muslims, no mullahs. No *muezzins*, please, singing on the midnight air.

Since Europeans got to North America, people have been called to their prayers by the peeling of bells. America has had and still has a bell culture. Bells for victories and weddings, bells for funerals, carillons for all occasions. The cacophony caused by mixing the peeling of bells with the wails made by a foreign man with a beard and a piece of cloth wrapped around his head strikes a sour note for Judeo-Christian Americans. The word *muezzin* is alien to the American ear. When Big Ben sounds it is calling all Anglo-Saxons, the blue eyed, fair skinned descendants of the Barons of Runnymead, direct heirs of the Great Charter of individual freedom. And let us not forget the Liberty Bell. In place of the ringing of the bells—the great, brass cast, reverberating sounds of the West, chiming, peeling, tolling, thundering—the Muslims proffer row upon row of robed, prostrate men on little rugs with their fannies stuck up in the air. Regardless of the non-stop talk extolling it, diversity has been a tough sell to a society whose national motto is *e pluribus unum*. Even groups which have not been associated with a foreign enemy, as Muslims are, have had to pay a significant penalty if their members chose to cling to a language other than English and religions which to the majority are threatening or alien or just peculiar. French- and German-speaking communities, Arcadians and Pennsylvania Dutch have only held on to their ways at the price of social isolation, with its attendant lack of opportunities and low income. The Hasidim of the New York City area have made much the same fate for themselves.

If there are two words in America which are uttered more frequently in public and less frequently in private than multiculturism and diversity, I don't know what they are. Politicians can't say enough for the two words. America has loudspeakers implanted in the walls of the terrarium insisting that multiculturalism and diversity are what makes it great. A nation is not a first-class, card-carrying democracy unless it is multiculturally diverse or diversely multicultural. America's welcoming, albeit fitfully, of people from

so many lands has made the nation special and quite won-
derful, although its lecturing of other nations to do the same
reinforces the impression on the other side of the glass curtain that America will not rest until it has turned the globe
into replicas of itself. The insistence on diversity puts a
country like Japan, which has a deep, irremediable, cultural
aversion to outsiders, in a painful position. Just as America
cannot be America without being a nation comprised of
people from diverse backgrounds, Japan would not be
Japan if it were.

Even so America hasn't much to brag about. Its diversity
was not intentional. It arose less from superior morality than
the nation being on an empty continent in dire need of
labor—the cheaper the better. There was money to be made
in diversity by steam ship companies, railroads, labor contractors importing strike-breakers, religious organizations
with their own agendas, and real estate speculators with
farm land to sell.

The Founding Fathers and their relatives did not envision the new republic as a heterogenous society. Circum-
stance and happenstance brought it about. After it had come
to be and people saw the good in it, it was made a trait
Americans were proud of, but they did not plan it that way
and they have repeatedly had misgivings about it. The
Japanese and Chinese were legally kept from citizenship or
owning land. For decades people from places such as India
or Indochina, people from anywhere within what the law
called the "Asiatic Barred Zone," could not get into not-so-
multicultural America.

The assumption of moral superiority by Americans on account of the country's multiculturalism astonishes people outside the hemisphere who can read, too. They know that Theodore Roosevelt said, "The question is whether we are to continue as a separate nation at all, or whether we are to become merely a huge polyglot boarding-house and counting-house, in which dollar hunters of twenty different nationalities scramble for gain, while each really pays his soul-allegiance to some foreign power." Nor is Theodore Roosevelt's question now a settled one and he some kind of long-ago bigot. His concerns over "soul-allegiance to some foreign power" are alive today, as they may apply to Muslims and to some Israeli sympathizers. Even while politicians and media personalities are carrying on about the glories of diversity, the country is ripped apart by arguments over immigration and its dangers, real or imagined, and the very real resentments over American people who cannot understand or speak English.

Muslims coming to the United States move into a society which, at the top most especially, is profoundly Anglo-Saxon in its political, legal and social values. Nothing has changed in the opinions of the America's top drawer rich from the time when Woodrow Wilson's ambassador to the Court of St. James, Walter Hines Page, wrote, "We Americans have to throw away our provincial ignorance, hang our Irish agitators and shoot our hyphenates, and bring up our children with reverence for English history and in awe of English literature."

Hyphenate was the less-than-flattering collective used in

the first quarter of the 20th century to refer to Irish- or African- or Japanese- or whomever-Americans. The only universally acceptable hyphenate was and is Anglo-Saxon; the price immigrants from diverse lands must pay for admittance is bleaching out their own cultural heritages. The place for the expression of non-Anglo culture, if there is one, is small and tenuous. In everyday life the practice of multiculturalism is limited to the incorporation of certain ethnic dishes in the American fast food menu—pizza, Tex-Mex, chop suey, popadam, tandoori, and yes, even falafel and pita. Once a year those identifying themselves with a non-American, non-name-brand national cultures are accorded a day on which they may parade and disport themselves in their native costumes, but you get one day and one day only. The rest of the time you will please keep your multicultural urges to yourself and within the bosom of your extended family or reference group.

If those have been the rules, most immigrants have been happy to observe them. The American business-commercial culture with its high standard of living and its toe-tapping glitz has been irresistible. If it was oppression, it was oppression by seduction, not by force. The American Way of Life or the American Dream has not wanted for people to take it up eagerly and make it their own. There have been holdouts to be sure, the people who use America, in Teddy Roosevelt's words, as a "counting-house, in which dollar hunters of twenty different nationalities scramble for gain," but two-thirds of the immigrants stayed and were happy to subordinate their respective cultural patrimonies in return for embracing Americanization.

Until the early 1960s Muslims had no part in the dramas of immigrant assimilation. There were next to none in the country and little was thought of them except that they were against Israel until, just as the civil rights upheaval was beginning to roil the nation, news began to creep out that the most feared segment of the American population, the black, male, criminal underclass, was taking up religion and that religion was Muhammadanism. Suddenly white America was introduced to the Nation of Islam by a thin, dangerously intelligent, ex-con, expositor of the new, foreign faith, a man who went under the disconcerting name of Malcolm X. Thus did the Americans learn of the Muslim religion, as taught by one who seemed to be announcing that Allah had sent a message to the frightful black men of the slums that it was payback time. There arose in the minds of the sedentary, white middle classes the old guilty nightmare of horrid, extra-black slaves, their grotesquely giant penises exposed and rigid, rushing the pillared plantation mansion, lusting after the blue-eyed you-know-whos.

The grand mufti of the Nation of Islam, the Honorable Elijah Muhammad, preached an anti-white doctrine which, however bizarre in its details, was what you might expect to hear from men at the bottom of the race pile. The more orthodox or traditionalist ministers of the Muslim religion elsewhere, without disavowing the peculiar American take on their religion, put a degree of distance between themselves and Black Muslimism, but Elijah Muhammad had defined the Muslim religion for Americans once and for all. Although he lived to become a much-loved public figure, when the world's heavyweight boxing champion, Cassius Clay, became Muhammad Ali and said, "I am not an American; I am a black man," it confirmed the worst fears of the non-Muslim millions.

The Muslim faith, like early Christianity, began to spread through the jails and penitentiaries. It is now well-entrenched in every prison in the country. Incarcerated Muslims are invisible and so, though the religion may be making significant inroads in the poorest part of the African-American population, it cannot be seen, but the religion has visibly percolated up through a wider social stratum. African-American people whose grandparents named their children after Theodore Roosevelt or Abraham Lincoln now give them Muslim names, even though they have not become Muslims themselves. Islam is used as a means of repudiation and as a tool for establishing a dignity and an identity independent of whites, which, though it has much to say for it, as a public relations ploy leaves something to be desired.

The penetration of Muslim religion and culture, particularly with its lines to the Middle East, has begun to have impacts on American life and politics. The small, impotent, and ignored left-wing intelligentsia aside, African-Americans are the first and largest group in the United States to turn away from Israel and throw their support to the Palestinian cause. This has done nothing to help the long term, slow deterioration of relations between African-Americans and the moneyed and highly placed segments of American Jewery. Allah may not be everywhere but He is around in more places than you might first imagine.

Awareness of the Muslim religion could not have come under poorer auspices than the black underclass, oil embargoes, withering accounts of the place of women in Islamic societies, stupid slobbering dictators, and the ceaseless Israeli-Palestinian conflict with its accompanying torrent of anti-Arab, anti Muslim propaganda. If Islam's sponsorship was bad, the timing of its entrance on the stage of American attention was as unlucky. It came as the class of people raised to fight the Cold War had their war pulled out from under them. Life without a world wide struggle to hurl themselves into was no life at all. They were like a set of teeth in an upper jaw looking for another set of teeth in a lower jaw to grind against. They soon found one.

The only thing lacking to raise the curtain on a cinema verite entitled *Jihad versus Crusade* was a Bernard of Clairvaux (1090–1153), the monk who, on March 31, 1146, in a field outside of Vezelay, France, preached a great crusade against the Muslim east to King Louis and the assembled French nobility. "Crosses, give us crosses!" the audience cried and one historian wrote that, "It was not long before all the stuff that had been prepared to sew into Crosses was exhausted; and Saint Bernard flung off his own outer garments to be cut up. At sunset he and his helpers were still stitching as more and more of the faithful pledged themselves to go on the crusade."

The American Bernard of Clairvaux is a couple of university professors, another Bernard whose last name is Lewis and Samuel P. Huntington, an academic sounder of the trumpet from Harvard. In 1990 Lewis wrote in an influential *Atlantic Monthly* article, "The Roots of Muslim Rage," that "We are facing a mood and movement far transcending the level of issues and policies and the governments that pursue them. This is no less than a clash of civilizations—the perhaps irrational but surely historic reaction of an ancient rival against our Judeo-Christian heritage, our secular present, and the world-wide expansion of both." On another occasion Lewis proclaimed that, "For them, [al Qaeda and, obviously, for Lewis, too] America is now the leader of Christendom, the ultimate enemy in the millennial struggle." Pass out the crosses, grab your spears and harken to Huntington declaring that, "The next world war, if there is one, will be a war between civilizations . . . A Confucian-Islamic military connection has . . . come into being, designed to promote acquisition by its members of weapons and the weapons technologies of the West . . . a central focus of conflict for the immediate future will be between the West and several Islamic-Confucian states." Huntington may have conflated Confucian states with a state of confusion, but in the unlikely event that peace breaks out in the Middle East, China gets dragged in as the back-up menace.

The academic Bernards of Clairvaux provided the intellectual scaffolding for the crusade. Others like George Bush, by preaching against the evil doers, popularized it without specifically saying that we are out on the moors playing hounds and Muslims. Less circumspect are loony tunes like Lt. Gen. William Boykin, caught running around to fundy congregations explaining to the people in the pews that he is a soldier in two armies, the American one and "the army of God [which] have been raised for such a time as this." According to this military wing-a-ding, when he has gone into battle against the Muslim infidel, "I knew my God was bigger than his. I knew that my God was a real God and his was an idol." However bigger General Boyton's may be than the heathen's, he is certain that, "We're a Christian nation . . . And the enemy is a guy named Satan." Whenever an American government official slips across the line and, like Boykin, lets crusader cat out of the bag, a mild repudiation from the White House is forthcoming, one which does not alleviate the suspicion that there may be a crackpot, religious underground in the American officer corps.

Outside the bubble, in the saner regions of the globe, the recrudescence of the wars of religion in America is another wedge making for two realities. America is dangerously religious; Europeans regard religion as something contra-indicated unless taken in small, measured doses. Old Europe has learned from its own history that faith is an intoxicant and the ship of state should not be driven under its influence. In America the Bush administration is making faith the basis of its policies. In Europe religious war is unthinkable; in the United States many think of little else.

In America the minister/politicians running the country and the fly-blown experts from the institutes, centers and foundations fixate on Wahabbism, the throat-cutting school of Muslim theology, but on the other side of the dome, those outside looking in see the Islamic Wahabbis, subsidized by the Saudi Arabians, matched by the Christian Wahabbis, backed by American money. The Muslim Wahabbis use terrorism to exercise their hatred. The Christian Wahabbis use warplanes and cruise missiles. To each according to his capacity to kill. Any American, Christian or Jew or luckless religious neutral, and any Muslim, regardless of age or occupation, is subject to being killed or maimed without notice. Unnoticed, too, are the Muslim deaths, of which there are by every count a great deal more, thanks to superior Judeo-Christian firepower. More deaths are to come, for faith-based war spares no one, neither infants nor the infirm. Since their theologies, Christian, Jewish, and Islamic, are irreconcilable, the faithful kill whoever believes otherwise, and, as they go about their bloody work, they doxologize the god they do hold in common: the God of War.

Religious hatred has been compounded by years of Muslim-baiting. Men like Lewis have taught that Islam is an inferior faith which has lost the race of history to the Judeo-Christian West and would do its adherents and the rest of the world a favor if it would dry up and blow away. It has become a fixed point of political doctrine that the Muslim religion is antagonistic to democracy, to science, to technology, to business, to liberty, to human dignity, and the entirety of the modern age. That should set any devotee's teeth on edge, on top of which the Muslim faithful must endure the lectures on the social and political arrangements of Islamic countries, on *sharia* law, on their gender roles, on how they dress, on how they vote

or don't, on how they raise their children, on their mar-
riages, on the deficiencies of the various schools of Islamic
theology. These denunciations, masquerading as scholarly
analysis and detached comment, would have won few converts to the American point of view even if unaccompanied
by invasions, coup d'états, embargoes, dispossessions, kid-
napings, assassinations, thefts, bombings, imprisonments,
armed incursions, torture, low intrigues, and armed inter-
ventions by the non-Muslim world, including by the
Soviet Union when it existed and by Russia now, and by
the capitalist West in its democratic and not-so-democratic
manifestations.

Since the Muslims have no armies worthy of the name,
they have done what some other underdogs have done:
They use their religious organizations as the center of their
resistence to aggression. The Irish used the Catholic Church
in such fashion against the English, as did the Poles against
the Communists. Mosques and *madrassas*, Islamic religious
schools, are used to recruit, organize and carry out terrorist
attacks against the anti-Islamic overdogs.

This is not the first time a religion has been the enemy of
the state in the history of the English-speaking people.
Much of the reign of Elizabeth I, in the 16th century, was
consumed by a struggle against a Roman Catholic underground intent on overthrowing the queen and recapturing
power in Britain. The Catholic party was backed at various
times and in various degrees by France and Spain, which
was then the most powerful nation in Europe.

In contests of this kind the question is always who is

loyal, who can be counted on, who is a traitor, and who is plotting assassination or terror. To ward off its clandestine attackers the government must violate the conscience of its citizens and pry into the souls of its people. In such struggles rights are disregarded wholesale, every norm is subject to abrogation. To protect herself and the realm Elizabeth leaned on the services of Sir Frances Walsingham (1530–1590), the minister who created and supervised networks of spies, agents, and what would be the modern equivalent of the Department of Homeland Defense. The country was turned into a Tudor version of a police state, replete with midnight arrests and torture.

The queen's position was made all the more precarious by the presence of so many Roman Catholics in her realm. Even Shakespeare is thought to have been one. America is lucky. The Muslim fraction of the population is small, so the network of police spies and undercover agents, sneaks, and informers does not have to be as wide as it was in Elizabethan England. Although in the 1950s, when there was an analogous situation with the Communists, who were far fewer in numbers than the Muslims of today, the domestic spy apparatus was very large indeed.

Queen Elizabeth and her ministers were forthright and public in their battles against Roman Catholicism, as contrasted to America with its over-developed ability to deny with its mouth the work of its hands. It insists that it is not waging a war of religion à la Bernard of Clairvaux, but such is not the opinion on the far side of the bubble where hundreds of millions of Muslims believe that America is out to destroy their faith or change it into something unrecognizable to them.

If the Americans have not learned it yet, and it is there in the history books for them to understand, wars of religion are next to unwinnable. Even when you think you have won one, when you have squashed every sign of the evil doers' faith, it is alive and invisible, a fact that will be clear enough when the next thunderbolt from below takes out an oil refinery, a grammar school, a hospital, a courthouse or a passenger train. Political, economic and territorial disputes are negotiable; religious wars are not. They only end when you stop fighting them.

22.
Hoax

"My administration, as has been the case with every president from President Roosevelt to President Reagan, is committed to the security and stability of the Persian Gulf . . . Our country now imports nearly half the oil it consumes and could face a major threat to its economic independence. Much of the world is even more dependent on imported oil and is even more vulnerable to Iraqi threats . . ."
—George Bush I, *August 8, 1990*

I F A PERSON STANDS next to a large wasp nest and repeatedly hits it with a stick, the person could consider what happens next an unprovoked wasp attack, if the person is so self-entranced that the person cannot discern cause and effect. Outside the dome, the person will be viewed with astonishment, consternation and, if the performance continues, with fear. As this puzzling individual goes on destroying the home of the now-maddened insects, they come at the person with suicidal fury, but he, as angered by the wasps' treatment of him as they of him, does not retreat even as his face is disfigured by venomous bites. He stands his ground killing his tormenters and being stung by them.

Fifteen years after George Bush, the elder, said he was going to war for "the security and stability of the Persian Gulf," the region has never been less secure and less stable.

A combination of money-bags political contributors, the Christian jihadists from the think tanks, the churches where they take Kool-Aid for communion, and the usual ethno-religious pressure groups are pressing the American government to take a wack at yet another wasp nest. One by one the Muslim nations of the Middle East are to be liberated and reconstituted as democracies under the motto of "Free Press, Free Market, Free Love" as the major energy companies gambol under sparkling fountains of rich, black crude oil.

From the outside looking in, the plan is a lunatic dream. Should Syria, Saudi Arabia, and Iran be favored with the same violent manumission accorded Iraq and Afghanistan, most of the oil fields will be so grievously injured the industrial powers will have to endure a generation of record-high energy prices. At the simplest, selfish level, these missionary ambitions will not pay out. As the first two invasions have shown, pre-war predictions of the ultimate costs are too low by orders of magnitude. In the practical realm, the persistent, nervous-Nelly focus on the security of the oil supply is misplaced. When the United States and the rest of the industrial world wants oil, it need only send empty tankers to the Middle East and, in exchange for money, the tankers will return full. What are the Muslim oil countries going to do with their oil? Sell it to someone else? There is no one else. Will they leave it in the ground? No. They want the money. Will they manipulate oil prices through OPEC (Organization of Petroleum Exporting Countries)? Yes. Will they succeed? No. Cartels fail to control prices because the cartel members end up cheating on each other.

To make the Middle East safe for oil export and foreign investment Islam must be de-fanged. That's the plan. Outside the dome, at least, they know that the grand reconfiguring of Islam will not come about through the op-ed offerings of modern day grub-streeters with more *sitzfleish* than gray matter, living the good life in their intellectual whore houses, which is what most think tanks are. The ditzes inside the dome may believe that their hermeneutics on the Koran will be taken seriously but Muslims won't. Even agnostics gag at George Bush and a bunch of American politicians and media personalities explaining the "true meaning" of Islam to a billion or so Muslims. Muslims and Muslims alone will decide what is their kind of fundamentalism, what is radical and what is moderate, if indeed such categories exist in the Islamic gestalt.

Unsolicited exegesis on other people's sacred texts is a species of Americans telling other people what is in their interest and how they should run their businesses. This "I know what's good for you"-ism extends past religion. Imperious American Pooh Bahs will announce on no authority at all that Iran has no legitimate use for atomic energy. It should rely on its oil for its energy needs. What would be the Department of State's answer to Iran if it gave America the same advice? Yet blithe officialdom has a piece of admonitory hokum on every topic for running the Arab nations. These non-stop pronunciamentos, beside irking those to whom they are directed, reveal a bottomless contempt for the people of the region.

If the conquest of the Middle East is to continue, it will

not yield a material advantage to the United States. The costs are so high that America will, in the end, be jacking up the price of gasoline on itself, yet it will not back out. The urge to make war in the Middle East is the urge to scratch the missionary itch. America is going to bring freedom, the thong, and private property to the Arabs and the Persians, whether they like it or not. American good works in the Middle East are reminiscent of the story of the Christian missionary in Africa who owned a Bible carved out of iron-wood. His ministry took the form of leading his converts down to the river for baptism by immersion. After the sacrament was administered and the heads of his converts broke the surface of the water, he smote them with his Bible, simultaneously sending his new congregants to heaven and pocketing such moneys as might have been on their persons. Small short-term gains for large long-term losses.

The two major disruptions of Middle Eastern oil supplies arose from Arab embargoes occasioned by the Israeli-American war against the Palestinians. There is no other wasp nest like this one. Just in passing, let it be noted that when it comes to hoaxes, political trompes d'oeil, misdirections, and conjuror's illusions, none compares to American neutrality in the Israeli war. The part played by Israel in deciding American policies is not discussed within the biosphere, but outside it is another story. Beginning with the Kennedy administration, the United States armed and financed the Israeli war machine, the most powerful in the region, a war machine which with its missiles and atomic bombs can defeat all the Arab nations one by one or all at the same time. So powerful is Israel that questions about Arab states' conceding Israel's "right to exist" are meaningless. Whatever Arab governments may think about Israel's right to exist, there is nothing they can do about Israel's existence except hope Israel does not bomb them.

With all its American-supplied military might, Israel is useless in maintaining Bush I's "security and stability of the Persian Gulf." It can destroy the oil fields, but it does not have enough soldiers to seize and hold them. In one of its ill-considered moves, Israel invaded Lebanon in the 1980s, ruined the place, but could not hold any of it against the never-ceasing attacks by Lebanese, Iraqi and Syrian bushwackers, guerillas, dry gulchers, irregulars, and terrorists. Outside of its own bailiwick, Israel, a total bust at multiculturalism and diversity, is not good for much beside limited or mass destruction. The Israelis are so hated in much of the world that even if they do have a few extra soldiers they cannot be used as peace keepers and/or nation builders in many of the places where such services are needed. Although this may not have been true forty or fifty years ago, today Israel, as an ally, is more of a drag than an asset.

Until the disintegration of Communist military power at the end of the 1980s, a convincing case could be made for arming Israel even though the arms were used against the Arabs, not the Reds. Continuing to build up Israeli military power after the collapse of Communism made the United States a co-belligerent in one of history's one-sided wars. It also was one of the powder trails leading to the dreadful explosion on the lower end of Manhattan. The slow, ceaseless Israeli taking of what, outside the terrarium, is considered Palestinian land is one of the reasons for 9/11. It is terrorism's unacknowledged predicate, the first, largest and least-spoken-of cause of Arab resentment.

Yet with each succeeding administration, regardless of which party has been in power, America has been Israel's co-belligerent. In the last half-century only the Eisenhower administration was "even-handed" in dealing with the Middle East, although presidents routinely strike the honest broker stance, which people under the dome believe while those on the other side of it simply accept because there is nothing else for them to do. Until it became too ludicrous even for the United States and Israel, American officials were under orders not to negotiate or even physically stay in the same room with anyone claiming to be a Palestinian representative. The Carter administration's ambassador to the United Nations was fired from his job for having a single, informal chat with a representative from the Palestinian Liberation Organization. Then came the peace process, a slow-motion dance by diplomatic zombies meant to convey the impression of progress toward an end to the dispute, carried out while the Israelis snipped off more little pieces of Palestinian real estate and planted them with squatters. In Israel it was called "making facts." Finally they made so many facts that the bombs started going off, killing Americans as well as Israelis.

In Tel Aviv the line has been that Israeli and American vital national interests are the same. Therefore every time an

Israeli pops off a Palestinian or bulldozes his domicile this is an advantage to the United States. No two nations have identical interests, least of all when one is a small, if very strong, regional power and the other is the mightiest nation there is. After 1990 or thereabouts, the interests of the two nations diverged, but they continued to walk in belligerent lock step. Anyone murmuring that while this may serve Israeli purposes it injured the United States interests, risked having the usual epithets flung at them. How two nations with such different fish to fry cooperated to the disadvantage of the more powerful one has been a mostly unexplored topic. Ordinarily, it is the big guy who takes advantage of the little guy. Not in this case, however.

Historian Kathleen Christison has researched how American policy is steered, and by whom. She has reviewed the background of top-rung American Middle Eastern officials. This, for instance, is what she says about key people in the Clinton administration, but the story is much the same for other administrations:

> The perspective of Clinton's aides appears to have been even more oriented toward Israel's interests. [Dennis] Ross and other principal members of the peace team, Aaron David Miller and Martin Indyk were all personally and emotionally committed to Israel. All had lived in Israel before entering government service; they often vacationed there. Miller and Indyk once told an interviewer that their personal and their professional involvement in the peace process

were so intertwined that they could not determine where one left off and the other began. Indyk said that the defining moment of his life came while he was living in Israel during the 1973 war when he decided to dedicate himself to helping resolve the conflict and concluded that U.S. involvement was critical both to ending the conflict and 'for Israel's defense.'

The accusation of dual loyalty has often been used by anti-Semites as a tool to attack all Jewish people and to allege conspiracies which do not exist. Nevertheless, in general divided loyalties do exist. There were disloyal German Americans in both the First and Second World Wars. The pro-British element in the American upper classes in the run up to World War I put the interests of another country in front of their own. There were disloyal Italian Americans in World War II, not many, but they were there. There were Americans of many stripes who put Communism over country. Nowadays the government is plucking Muslim Americans out of their beds and charging them with serving the interests of another cause to the detriment of their country. Dual loyalty exists, sometimes out in the open and sometimes hidden, but either way the possibility of its playing a role in any conflict, but especially a quasi-religious war, cannot be excluded. No one knows the secrets of the human heart but, looking at the record of a Ross or an Indyk in the Clinton administration, or of a Richard Perle, the neocon White House habitué, or Deputy Secretary of Defense Paul Wolfowitz in the Bush II administration, one asks if, when these men take the oath of office, are they committing perjury?

However arrived at, the consequence of Middle Eastern policy is that the nation is under lock-up, like a penitentiary. Daily life is standing on lines, searches, delays, petty humiliations, questionings, and intrusions by police forces and security organizations, notable for not getting it right, or, in the idiom of the day, never "connecting the dots." Cultivating a siege mentality may keep the Republican Party in office, but the guards, fences, police lines, and security procedures will not protect people inside the terrarium. Regardless of how much is spent stopping it, terrorist contraband will get into the country. Some of it can be stopped but not all of it, and one failure can equal a thousand deaths. Law enforcement in the United States cannot keep drugs out of penitentiaries where inhabitants live in steel cages. They cannot keep drugs and guns out of grammar schools. It follows that they are not and will not be able to keep guns and worse out of the United States. In its fear the nation is like a man who bricks up the windows and doors of his house to keep the burglars out, and they slip down the air conditioning duct. How many bombs and anthrax vials are kept out is problematic, but we know for certain the fresh ideas and the contacts between people from which springs invention, creation, amity, and prosperity are excluded. A cost-benefit analysis of what America has done to itself would show that the protection program is all cost and no benefit.

Previously, when the government asked people to sacrifice,

it was explained that it was "for the duration of the emergency." People spoke of "when the war is over." In this one
no American official refers to "after the war." What they say
is that "9/11 changed everything," meaning that the era of
cops, body armor, orange alerts, barricades, magnetometers,
national lock-downs, and muffled rumors of nocturnal
arrests and disappeared persons is permanent.

Abroad America has got itself a foreign policy it does not
have the heft to swing. Armed service people in dark rooms
staring at computer monitors and typing orders to weapons
of mass destruction will not cut it, but there is nothing else
for it. America has many people but few soldier boys and
soldier girls. Native born Americans will not do stoop labor
in the lettuce fields, they will not do the dirty jobs in hospitals, they will not clean public toilets or join the Army and
go to war. The United States cannot recruit enough soldiers
to do the army's cooking, let alone endure the indefinite and
dangerous duty demanded for the subjugation of
Afghanistan and Iraq.

On the other side of the great greenhouse they see an
America that is broke and in debt, borrowing ever larger
sums to hire foreigners to do ever more critical work.
Without enough Americans to fight its preemptive wars to a
victory, the United States has been forced to canvass the
globe for fighters. It rents soldiers from down-at-the-heel
mini-states, begs for them from the French and the Germans,
borrows from the Brits, and pays an assortment of merce-
naries, condottiere, Bashi-Bazooks, and underemployed
Foreign Legionnaires to do the fighting its own people will

not do. Outside the ant farm they measure the length of the growing difference between America's grasp and its reach.

Outside the terrarium looking in, it is plain to see that the nation, which Franklin Roosevelt called the "arsenal of democracy," no longer makes its own shoes. America no longer makes its own living. The greatest threat to the oil supply is not war or embargo but a demand by Arab suppliers that they be paid in euros instead of dollars, because every year America buys more from people abroad than it sells to them, and then borrows the money to pay for its purchases from the people it buys from. It is now the biggest debtor in the history of the world. Like many another debtor, it owes so much money its creditors are petrified of what might happen if they foreclosed on the mortgage. Step by step, America is losing its moral power, its cultural power, and its economic power, leaving it to depend on its military power, the crudest, the least subtle, the least dependable kind of power. Bit by bit, America leads less by example and ideals and gets its way by squeezing, by fraud, by intimidation, and by hectoring its friends.

If a nation won't go out gang-banging with it, George Bush knocks it off the friends list. But over two centuries America has banked a lot of good will and gratitude. Countries it has written off have not reciprocated. The world is not out to get America.

Inside the bubble the failure of America's allies to do what they are told is seen as the ill will and envy of fair-weather friends and summer soldiers. A special scorn is reserved for the French, America's oldest friend without whose fleet

George Washington could not have won the Battle of York-
town nor the Revolutionary War. Snide remarks and curled
lips are tossed in the direction of the French, who gave the
United States the Statue of Liberty and who have been the
most enthusiastic admirers of America for more than two
hundred years. When England had no use for Benjamin
Franklin, France idolized him, as Voltaire and Rousseau and
the other philosophes of the French Enlightenment idolized
the American Dream even before America knew it had one.
It was a Frenchman, Alexis de Tocqueville, who wrote the
most influential and widely quoted study of American politics, society, and character. The French recognized jazz as an
important art form before the Americans themselves did, as
they recognized Jerry Lewis before the Americans, who still
have not completely come to grips with that one. Of all the
people of the world, none have loved America as long or as
passionately as the French.

Aside from being French, the greatest error the French
have made in American eyes is reining in their own touchy
nationalism enough to join in the building of the European
Union, Europe's greatest political accomplishment in an
eon of historical time. For much of the world the EU has
become a model and marker for cooperation and joint
enterprise. For America, it, like other, new, laboriously
established multinational institutions covering every topic
from war crimes to environmental protection, is a threat to
"the American Century," the phrase coined by Henry Luce
during World War II.

America is not over but the American Century is, a state-

ment of fact which sends neocons into star spangled
apoplexy. The enormous preponderance of wealth, technology and power which was once America's has been
shrinking. Outside the dome, the fact that others have more
doesn't make America less, but inside, where trade, sports,
and science are a form of war without shooting, whatever is
good news for somebody else is, axiomatically, bad news for
Americans. Any plus for them is a minus for us; any accomplishment outside the dome is a threat, a setback, a defeat
for USA! USA! USA!

The EU, which has caught up with the USA, gives Bush,
Cheney, and their circle such quiet fits they stick out a sur-
reptitious foot to trip Europe whenever the chance presents
itself. Although it will be many decades yet before daily life
in China is as comfortable as it is in Milwaukee, Wisconsin,
they are alarmed that the Yellow Peril is on its way to
catching up. The richer the nation, the higher the standard
of living, the more there is to lose. Nothing guarantees
peace like prosperity. Yet the un-realpolitik of the people
who run the country has brought America into a perpetual
state of bristly, under-the-surface hostility toward others
and a neocon neo-isolationism. For a nation dependent on
the good will of strangers to pay its bills, it is a self-defeating
posture.

Inside and outside the dome America is a stand-alone,
one-of-a-kind nation. The knowledge of what America has
been and what it is hoped it will be again induces the outsiders to cut America a lot of slack. They take rudeness off
America, insulting little asides, they take being skipped over

in the making of decisions which concern them, too, and they take gratuitous cock-of-the-walk arrogance. They take a lot of crap because there is much residual respect and affection for America, because of their dependence on American power, because they sell America a lot of merchandise, and because they fear they may lose the money they have lent America.

On their side of the glass, Americans think they are God's special gift to mankind. They invented everything worth inventing and have done everything worth doing. They invented blue jeans and mass production and the atom bomb, and if they could not have done the last without the help of a university full of European refugees from Hitler's fascism, they have forgotten about it or it doesn't count.

The most important thing America invented, America believes, was freedom and democracy, and like the gift of fire they are going to pass democracy on to the rest of the world which does not have it. According to myth, after Prometheus filched fire from Zeus to give it to human beings, he was punished by being chained to the side of a cliff where, everyday, an eagle—not an American one, let us hope—came and ate his liver, which grew back so that the eagle could return the next day for another wholesome well-balanced meal.

When America, uninvited, bestows democracy on another country it gets its liver pecked. Turnkey democracies, franchised like Burger Kings and KFCs, fail. South America and the Caribbean are crawling with these mutant, teratological democracies. Yet anybody opening a fast food democracy featuring dishes on the menu not approved by the American franchisers will find themselves closed down lickety split. Should the day ever come that an Afghanistan or an Iraq gets some kind of rickety democracy up and running, and should it vote in an Islamic state or limit foreign investment or vote out Citicorp and Halliburton, what would happen? Humans might have accepted fire from Prometheus but America's pre-fabbed governments, its gift of fire, barely flickers and gives off no heat. Democracy is not given by one nation to another. Every society, every nation which adopts it does it in its own way, based on its own social customs and beliefs.

America may no longer be a model democracy, but it is a democracy. Americans have had many years to take the political steps to stop or redirect what its government has been doing in the Middle East. They have not done so, and in questions of this kind the old bromide holds true: silence is consent. Thus in the final reckoning America has itself to blame for the terrorist attacks. Long before the terrorists bombed New York, America was bombing Arabs. This is a hard idea to accept. After the assassination of John F. Kennedy, Malcolm X was almost run out of public life and may have been murdered for saying that America's chickens had come home to roost. In other words, he believed that Kennedy's attempts to assassinate Fidel Castro had resulted in his own death.

The broad public did not know about the attempts on Castro's life, but what has been done in the Middle East was done with the public's knowledge and it was done over a

generation or more. Americans had many years to organize
politically to force a change in course, but they did not do it.
They were told to back their presidents and they did. They
were lied to about this and that and the other, but lies, like
other forms of garbage, are biodegradable. After a while they
disintegrate, leaving the truth out there for anybody to see who
wants to see. If blame attaches, it is on the American people.

You are not to defame or libel the American people. We
treat The People the way we once treated The King. If government did anything wrong, it was not The King's fault. It
was his evil, wicked advisors. If The King only knew, The
King would not let it happen. In actuality The King was a
jerk who surrounded himself with flatterers and scheming
miscreants who shamefully manipulated him. It would be sac-
rilege to say that The People are jerks, but they have allowed
themselves to be surrounded by flatterers who have turned
their brains into a complacent jelly. They hear nothing but
flattery. Their politicians, their anchor men, their corporate
advertisers, their clergy, their professors, every public voice
extolls them. They are praised for their standard of living,
for how many cars they have per capita, for how long they
can hope to live, for how many Big Macs they will enjoy over
an average lifetime, for how many things they own. Flattery
being irresistible, the people believe it but, as grandmother
says, when you stick out your chest, your brain stops
working.

Or blame the media for Americans' acquiescence to what
their elected officials have brought down on them. Everybody blames everything on the media—the liberals, the

reactionaries, the elites, the levelers, whoever it is and whatever it is, it's the media's fault. There is a reason. Taken as a whole the mass media seldom rises to the level of deplorable trash, but it is also true that there is no mass audience in America for anything better, and anyone who offers a higher quality will go broke trying. Hence CNN has two services, an American brain-candy service for morons and another service for viewers on the far side of the dome. Even the brain-candy service has so few viewers it scarcely qualifies as a mass medium.

Even though most of the mass media disseminates government propaganda and human interest cheerleading in place of information, Americans cannot cop a plea because the mass media kept the truth from them. It didn't.

If Americans had wanted to know they could have known. The case of the Germans in Nazi times is on point. After a certain amount of time they had to know. They weren't innocently ignorant, because the mass murders by the Nazis went on too long, for three or four years. The American government has been harvesting the Middle Eastern grapes of wrath for a generation and not making a secret of it, either. As lousy as the mass media may be, there was enough news about what was transpiring, year after year, to get the gist of what was happening. Besides, as George Bush is correct in reminding his people, America is still a democracy and there is free communication. No American can truthfully say that they could not find out what was going on, least of all now when there has never been more information, more easily obtained.

In the end the hoax is a self-hoax. What is a hoax, anyway? The word derives from hocus-pocus, the conjuror's mysterious-sounding verbal formulary for baffling, befuddling, and bemusing the suckers. Suckers are less victims than aggravating, needy-greedy, concupiscent people living the upscale life in fine new houses built on old farm land. Like most confidence schemes, the Middle East adventure depends on the cooperation of the mark. Millions allowed themselves to be gulled. The call went out to support the president and they did, one president after another, and they believed every lying, dissembling one: Kennedy, Johnson, Nixon, Ford, Carter, Reagan, Bush I, Bill Clinton, and now, the worst of the bunch, Bush II. No questions asked, no questions answered, just listen to the speech and get the old red, white, and blue pumping through the veins.

Whoever is in the White House, the biosphere stays closely sealed. If the air locks are not opened, America's friends will continue to recede and find new paths of their own. In the Middle East the turmoil and the terror waxes and wanes. It has a certain pattern. Herky-jerky armed incursions, optimistic predictions, long-range excursions by cruise missiles, and from time to time the Muslims and Arabs will throw a few punches of their own and occasionally terror will connect with a stinger like the World Trade Center. But America has a goodly supply of skyscrapers and more than a sufficiency of people for the occasional catastrophe. It can afford to sacrifice a few of each on the altar of whatever name the politicians happen to be giving the cause at the moment of impact.

In reality the future will be the one thing nobody predicted. No one could have known when the Crusades began that in the year 1204 Pope Innocent III would declare a crusade against his fellow Christians, the Albigensian heretics in southern France. The lords and barons of the north fell on the Albigensians with a battle cry which anticipates the effect of modern weapons of mass destruction: "Kill them all and let God sort them out later." That is what they did and the Albigensians were extirpated. Not enough of them are left for us to know what they believed and how they lived.

Another message with better counsel comes from the same distant time of Christian, Jewish and Arab hatred and fear. It is a verse from the pseudo-Gospel of Barnabas, thought to have been written in the early 1300s, a work in which parts of the Bible are mixed with parts of the Koran:

"As God liveth, even as the fire burneth dry things and converteth them into fire, making no difference between olive and cypress and palm; even so our God hath mercy on every one that worketh righteously, making no difference between Jew, Scythian, Greek or Ishmaelite."

George Bush has got more of Innocent III than of Barnabas in him. These snippets from one of his speeches give a whiff of the missioneering triumphalism which rules his administration:

"In our conflict with terror and tyranny, we have an unmatched advantage, a power that cannot be resisted, and that is the appeal of freedom to all mankind . . . If the greater Middle East joins the democratic revolution that has reached much of the world, the lives of millions in that region will be bettered . . . Our part . . . is to ally ourselves with reform wherever it occurs . . ."

Like his fellow Judeo-Christian warriors Bush is of the convert 'em or kill 'em school, which, history shows, can induce genuine conversions. The tip of a sword pricking the tender skin of the throat has helped to turn more than one heathen into a true believer. Both the Christian and Muslim religions owe a lot to coercion.

So does democracy. Forced conversion was tried in Vietnam, when President Lyndon Johnson was supposed to have explained that the proper procedure for the conversion of infidels was to "grab 'em by the balls and their hearts and minds will follow." Hundreds of thousands of balls were grabbed but, alas, few hearts and minds were attached.

Life and history, however, are devilishly mischievous. No sooner had the Yankee brutes packed up their weapons of mass destruction and bugged out for home than Vietnamese opinion began to swing in America's favor. The contra-cyclical movement continues but if there is a lesson there, it is lost on Washington.

The forced conversion of the population of a single country is no small project. Running most of the world under the holy water spigot is an undertaking for Texans who can see long distances across their arid, flat state. Call it vision or having visions, but on hot days the heat rising from the range forms hologram pictures of family values, basic integrity, and Amber alerts. It is then that febrile brains entertain thoughts on converting the world.

The last supra-national faith to use force, guile, sex and

money to convert everybody else was the Soviet Union, through the instrumentality of its Comintern, the office of international subversion and domination. At first people joined the red church, but then Marxist-Leninist became the god that failed. Communism was revealed to be little more than androgynously steroidal East German women swimmers, the Yugo, the Warsaw Pact, the Gulag, 150 million vodka-swilling alcoholics, and Chernobyl.

It has been said that the big difference between the quondam superpowers is that the United States lags the old Soviet Union by about forty years. Be that as it may, American athletes are flunking urine tests with record-breaking distinction. American cars may not be Yugos, but Americans won't buy them. In a war between the Warsaw Pact and the Coalition of the Willing, could either side win? There is no American Gulag but George Bush is set to negotiate with Fidel Castro for room to expand his Guantanamo Bay concentration camp. They may not drink vodka but add up the drunks and the Americans stoned on prescription drugs and recreational substances, and what percentage of the USA's population is perpetually intoxicated? Thirty? Forty? But no Chernobyl, just blackouts.

The first resort is war; the second, if you have run out of soldiers, is peace. In any event, as George Bush, who has uttered more benedictions than the Pope, would say, "God Bless you."